Generative AI and Large Language Models: An Overview of Current Trends and Terminology in the Field

Muslum Yildiz
Dr. Fatih Hattatoglu
Mustafa Erdogan
Dr. Mustafa Erboga

"Generative AI has the potential to change the world in ways that we can't even imagine. It has the power to create new ideas, products, and services that will make our lives easier, more productive, and more creative. It also has the potential to solve some of the world's biggest problems, such as climate change, poverty, and disease. The future of generative AI is bright, and I'm excited to see what it will bring."

Bill Gates
Former CEO of Microsoft

TABLE OF CONTENTS

TABLE OF CONTENTS

PREFACE

AUTHORS

CHAPTER 1

INTRODUCTION TO GENERATIVE AI

    1.1 UNDERSTANDING GENERATIVE AI: CONCEPTS AND MECHANISM

        1.1.1 Captivating Curiosity: The Intrigue of Generative AI

        1.1.2 In the realm of Artificial Intelligence, Where does Generative AI stand?

        1.1.3 What is Generative AI?

    1.2. DISCRIMINATIVE AND GENERATIVE TECHNIQUE

CHAPTER 2

DIVERSE CAPABILITIES OF GENERATIVE AI

    2.1 NAVIGATING GENERATIVE AI'S DIVERSE CAPABILITIES

        2.2.1 Writing, Reading And Chatting

    2.2 DALL-E 2: A CREATIVE LEAP IN GENERATIVE AI

CHAPTER 3

LARGE LANGUAGE MODELS (LLMs)

    3.1 EXPLORING LARGE LANGUAGE MODELS (LLMs)

    3.2 BENEFITS AND RISKS OF USING LARGE LANGUAGE MODELS

    3.3 SELECTING THE RIGHT LARGE LANGUAGE MODEL

    3.4 THE INNER WORKINGS OF LLMs: UNVEILING THE MECHANISM

        3.4.1 KING OF AI ARCHITECTURES: TRANSFORMERS

            3.4.1.1 ANN

            3.4.1.2 RNN

            3.4.1.3 LSTM

            3.4.1.4 GRU

            3.4.1.5 TRANSFORMERS

CHAPTER 4

ADVANCED TECHNIQUES IN LARGE LANGUAGE MODELS

    4.1 RETRIEVAL-AUGMENTED LANGUAGE MODELS (RALMs)

    4.2 RETRIEVAL-AUGMENTED GENERATION (RAG)

    4.3 REINFORCEMENT LEARNING FROM HUMAN FEEDBACK (RLHF)

    4.4 PROMPT ENGINEERING: FACILITATING USER AND AI INTERACTION

CHAPTER 5

CHALLENGES AND LIMITATIONS IN GENERATIVE AI

    5.1 HALLUCINATIONS

    5.2 CONTEXT WINDOWS

CHAPTER 6

GENERATIVE AI'S IMPACT ON ECONOMIC EVOLUTION

    6.1 THE ROLE OF GENERATIVE AI IN ECONOMIC EVOLUTION

    6.2 COST INTUITION OF GENERATIVE AI

CONCLUSION

SUGGESTED READINGS: Articles published by the authors

REFERENCES

PREFACE

Welcome to the captivating world of Generative AI, where imagination meets cutting-edge technology in a symphony of creativity and innovation. We invite you to embark on an exhilarating journey with us as we explore the fascinating landscape of Generative AI in our book, "**Generative AI and Large Language Models: An Overview of Current Trends and Terminology in the Field.**"

This book unveils the enchanting realm where technology converges with imagination, creating a fusion of art and science that promises to redefine the future.

Generative AI, often likened to modern wizardry, has swiftly showcased magical capabilities, marrying the art of creation with the precision of mathematical sciences. As we navigate the chapters, we unravel the layers of this fascinating technology—grasping its potential, uncovering diverse applications, and deciphering the intricate mathematics and statistics that underpin it.

Featuring insights from luminaries like Andrew Ng, who draws parallels between AI's evolution and historical technological advancements, the book provides a historical context and a glimpse into AI's potential societal impact. Not engaging with questions about AI attaining consciousness or the emergence of Artificial General Intelligence (AGI), the book opens doors to endless possibilities and reflections on AI's future.

This book delves into the current advancements in productive artificial intelligence, specifically examining the societal impacts of pioneering technologies such as ChatGPT and DALL-E 2 and the innovations they enable. It thoroughly explores the scholarly articles on large language models existing in the literature, which form the foundation of these innovations. The book aims to clarify these technologies' terminology and underlying mechanisms, presenting the theoretical and practical underpinnings in an accessible manner.

Furthermore, it offers a detailed analysis of the potential impacts of productive artificial intelligence on global productivity and the economy. This analysis assumes the potential of these technologies to contribute trillions of dollars to the economy. The book emphasizes the importance of staying current and competitive in a rapidly evolving technological world, highlighting the necessity of proactive engagement with artificial intelligence technologies. It calls for concrete actions in this field, underlining the urgency of adapting to and leveraging these advancements.

Approaching the conclusion, we consider the delicate balance between caution and optimism that AI presents. This book encourages readers to embrace a proactive mindset, positioning technology as a tool and a partner in shaping a more prosperous world.

In essence, this book is a guide, a reflection, and a call to action, inviting all to partake in the wonders and realities of Generative AI. To provide reference to its content, it is worth noting that the book draws from over a hundred sources, primarily academic articles, with most of these sources dating back to the year 2023. All the authors have been teaching in this field for an extended period, closely tracking the latest developments, which you can also see in the articles shared at the end of the book.

Welcome to a world where the marvels of **Generative AI and Large Language Models** constantly redefine the boundaries of possibility.

AUTHORS

Muslum YILDIZ

With over five years of expertise, Müslüm Yıldız is a seasoned **Deep Learning and Computer Vision Instructor** renowned for his proficiency in technologies such as **Deep Learning, Computer Vision**, NLP, **Generative AI, Speech Recognition**, and **Reinforcement Learning**. Having made significant contributions in the USA, UK, and Germany, he has played pivotal roles as a Deep Learning and Computer Engineer, Product Owner, and educator.

Muslum Yildiz is a crucial figure in a **US-based** company's education division, specializing in **Deep Learning, NLP,** and **Computer Vision**. His teaching portfolio has recently expanded to include **Reinforcement** and **Generative AI**, showcasing a commitment to advancing tech education through innovative methods and curriculum development.

On the academic front, Muslum Yildiz is nearing completion of a **Ph.D. in Information and Document Management** from Ankara University. His research focuses on applying Deep Learning, Computer Vision, Speech Recognition, and NLP to bridge the gap between academic theory and practical application.

Dr. Fatih HATTATOGLU

With a **Ph.D. in Engineering**, Dr. Fatih Hattatoglu has leveraged his robust background in programming and accumulated over three years of experience in **machine learning**, **statistics**, **tableau**, and **data science**. Additionally, he has a rich academic background and has served as an educator at a reputable university for 17 years. Throughout his teaching career, he has taught thousands of students and shared his deep knowledge of these cutting-edge technologies. His contributions to the academic world have been highly successful and recognized, shaping many young minds and future professionals in the field.

He is proficient in **machine learning** and **deep learning algorithms**. As a lifelong learner and a passionate academic, he prides himself on understanding the principles behind these algorithms and staying updated with the latest advancements and publications in AI.

Over the years, he has developed a solid knowledge of machine learning techniques. He has successfully applied them in many areas, leading to several academic papers on artificial neural networks. His role as an instructor has allowed him to effectively disseminate this knowledge and mentor students, thereby playing a significant part in the growth of future AI experts.

He is highly motivated to continuously enhance his problem-solving, time-management, and creative thinking skills, which he believes are indispensable in addressing complex challenges in Information Technology. His passion for research and commitment to staying at the forefront of AI technologies make him an enthusiastic and dedicated individual. He continually strives to explore and innovate in AI, ensuring that his students are always at the cutting edge of technology.

Mustafa ERDOGAN

Embarking on a dynamic career that spans continents, Mustafa Erdogan has made significant contributions in the USA, UK, and Germany, assuming pivotal roles as a **Machine Learning Engineer**, Product Owner, and dedicated educator. As a fervent **Data Scientist**, he channels his passion toward utilizing data to drive impactful business decisions and specializes in the intricate domains of network analysis and visualization. With over six years of hands-on experience, his expertise extends across Artificial Intelligence, **Machine Learning**, **Deep Learning**, and **Natural Language Processing** (NLP), leaving an indelible mark on academia, healthcare, and various business sectors.

He has a proven track record in data analytics in crafting robust data regression models, employing predictive data modeling techniques, and dissecting data mining algorithms to unearth profound insights. His mastery in **Machine Learning** shines through, and he effortlessly navigates tools such as **Python**, web scraping, Google Sheets, Tableau, and Power BI.

Beyond the tech landscape, he seamlessly transitions into the role of a dynamic health manager, boasting an impressive 20 years of industry experience within health institutions. With a robust academic background in health management, he endeavors to inject current and innovative approaches into health management literature through his ongoing studies. His commitment to pushing the boundaries of healthcare practices underscores his multifaceted impact at the intersection of technology and health management.

Dr. Mustafa ERBOGA

Dr. Mustafa ERBOGA is a recognized **Data Science expert** with over five years of experience. Skilled in **Deep Learning, Computer Vision, NLP, Generative AI**, and **Machine Learning**, he has made notable contributions in the USA and Germany, establishing himself as a distinguished industry professional.

ERBOGA's expertise lies in data science, particularly in exploratory data analysis using tools like **Machine Learning, Deep Learning**, SQL, Power BI, and Tableau. He has published over 30 medical articles and completed 20 projects, showcasing his statistical analysis and research proficiency. His experience spans healthcare and education, demonstrating his ability to solve real-world problems effectively.

Adept at building robust **Machine Learning** and **Deep Learning** models with Scikit-Learn, Keras, and TensorFlow, he also has experience deploying models with Streamlit and AWS Sagemaker. ERBOGA's comprehensive skill set and international experience make him a valuable asset in technology and education, standing out in Deep Learning and **Computer Vision**.

CHAPTER 1
INTRODUCTION TO GENERATIVE AI

INTRODUCTION TO GENERATIVE AI

In 1981, **Shel Silverstein** wrote the poem "**The Homework Machine**" in his book "**A Light in the Attic**". It was a book with children's poems and an exciting work that foreshadowed today's advanced computing technologies, such as large language models (LLM). The poem amusingly describes an imaginary machine that will easily do a child's homework. Silverstein describes the machine in these words: "*Put your homework in, then put in a dime, press the button, and in ten seconds, your homework comes out fast and clean.*" This reflects the desire for an automated and easy solution for everyday tasks, especially those that are considered tedious or laborious, such as homework.

However, Silverstein's machine, although attractive, is humorously flawed. It produces false results, "*Here it is - 'nine plus four?*' and the answer is *'three'*." This poem represents the limitations and shortcomings of early technological expectations (Figure 1).

Now, decades later, this fanciful vision is finding resonance in the field of large language models such as **ChatGPT**. These models represent a giant technological leap forward, capable of understanding and producing human-like text using extensive data and sophisticated algorithms (Lund & Agbaji, 2023). They fulfill many functions, including educational tasks, like the fantastic homework machine. However, unlike Silverstein's creation, which makes mistakes in simple arithmetic, today's LLMs strive for higher accuracy and contextual relevance, but only with their limitations and areas for improvement.

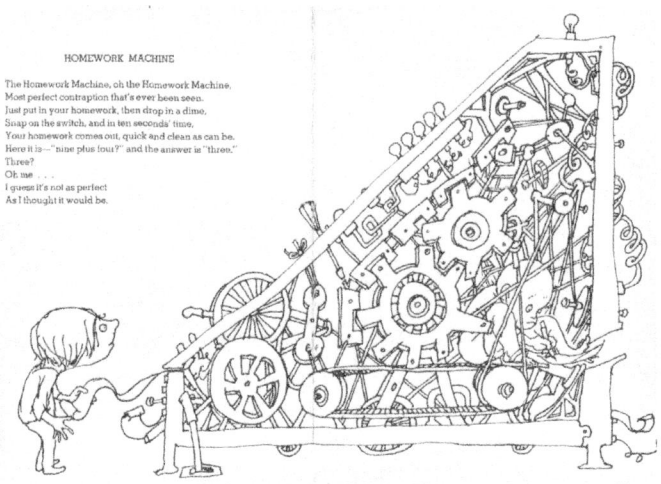

Figure 1: Homework Machine
Source: Silverstein, S. (1981)

This evolution from Silverstein's "**Homework Machine**" to today's LLMs is a technological journey and a story of human desire and creativity. Silverstein's poetry captures an enduring human desire for technological aids in everyday life, blended with imagination and foresight. The machine's dream can be seen as a more sophisticated, real-world realization of its cheerful tone and imaginative design, finding a surprising counterpart in developing LLMs.

From this perspective, Silverstein's work transcends its time and demonstrates that artistic imagination can foreshadow and inspire real-world technological advances. Now, as we turn our attention to **Generative AI**, we will see how it goes beyond just language and ventures into broader realms of creativity and innovation. Let us delve into a journey that goes beyond the limits of language intelligence and explores the various aspects of **Generative AI**.

1.1 UNDERSTANDING GENERATIVE AI: CONCEPTS AND MECHANISM

1.1.1 Captivating Curiosity: The Intrigue of Generative AI

In recent times, the capabilities of ChatGPT and DALL-E have unfolded as a surprising revelation, leaving a lasting impression on many of us. The advancements in generative artificial intelligence have sparked wonder and significantly eased the burden of our daily tasks, especially for those grappling with time constraints.

Much like the magic woven by a skilled wizard, these generative AI advancements go beyond mere technological breakthroughs; they represent a paradigm shift in how we interact with and leverage artificial intelligence. The wonder elicited by these advancements stems from their ability to surpass conventional expectations, presenting innovative solutions to long-standing challenges.

For individuals navigating the pressures of time, the impact of generative AI becomes especially pronounced. The technology acts as a catalyst, significantly easing the burden of our daily responsibilities. Whether streamlining communication, enhancing creativity, or optimizing problem-solving, generative AI is valuable for those seeking efficiency in their routines.

The capabilities of **ChatGPT** and **DALL-E** are emblematic of the broader landscape of generative AI, where curiosity meets innovation. This recent surge in wonder-inducing technologies captures our fascination. It marks a transformative period in navigating the intersection of artificial intelligence and our daily lives, much like the bewitching effects of a magician's spell.

There has been a noticeable surge in interest regarding generative AI, as reflected in the substantial increase in Google searches since late 2022. The introduction of ChatGPT in late 2022, perceived as the catalyst for a new technological revolution, has notably heightened curiosity. The public's growing fascination with generative AI is evident in the remarkable rise in searches on Google, indicating a widespread recognition of the technology's potential and impact across different areas. This Increased attention is likely fueled by advancements in the field, practical applications, and the release of influential generative AI models. As generative AI progresses, its growing visibility underscores its significance and the anticipation of future developments (Figure 2).

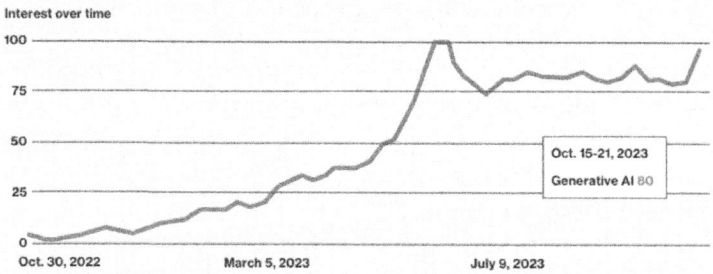

Figure 2: Searches for the term "generative AI" by Google users
Source: MIT Technology Review Insights (2023).

The emergence of generative AI has transformed how we interact with information and creativity. One of the most notable changes is how we summarize lengthy texts. This technology can distill extensive documents into concise, digestible summaries, making information consumption more efficient.

Moreover, generative AI has shifted our approach to online search. Gone are the days when we relied solely on keyword-based searches on platforms like Google. Now, we can ask direct questions, which has proven more intuitive and practical, seemingly overshadowing traditional search engines. This evolution in search methodologies is a convenience and a significant leap in accessing and processing information.

Another groundbreaking application of generative AI is in coding and software development. Developers, often challenged by the complexity of reading and writing intricate code, now have a powerful tool at their disposal. Generative AI can understand and generate complex code within seconds, dramatically increasing efficiency and reducing the learning curve for new programmers.

One of the most exciting advancements is in the field of digital art. We can create original, artist-quality images tailored to our preferences and styles with tools like **DALL-E**. This capability unlocks new realms of creativity and personal expression, democratizing art creation in unprecedented ways.

Furthermore, generative AI has ventured into the literary world, displaying the ability to write poetry and novels. This showcases technical proficiency and a level of creativity and understanding that many thought was exclusive to human intellect.

So, what is the driving force behind all these remarkable innovations? The answer lies in the realm of **Generative AI**. This technology is not just a tool but a paradigm shift, offering a glimpse into a future where AI's role transcends conventional boundaries, blending creativity, efficiency, and intelligence in ways we are only beginning to comprehend.

With this book, we aim to explore the depths and breadths of generative AI, unraveling its capabilities, potential applications, and the profound impact it is poised to have on our world.

1.1.2 In the realm of Artificial Intelligence, Where does Generative AI stand?

Artificial Intelligence (AI) is the overarching domain in technological advancements, encompassing various techniques and methodologies to enable machines to mimic human intelligence. Within this broad field exists a structured hierarchy where specific subfields are nested within each other, much like **a set of Russian dolls**. **Machine Learning**, **Deep Learning**, and the more recent and rapidly evolving **Generative AI** are at the core of this hierarchy.

This hierarchy (Figure 3) shows how AI, Machine Learning, Deep Learning, and Generative AI are connected, each being more advanced than the last. Machine Learning allows computers to learn from data. Deep Learning goes further, handling large volumes of data and driving many modern AI applications like speech recognition, image processing, and autonomous vehicles. Generative AI, at the top, not only processes data but also creates new, original content, thereby expanding the creative capabilities of machines.

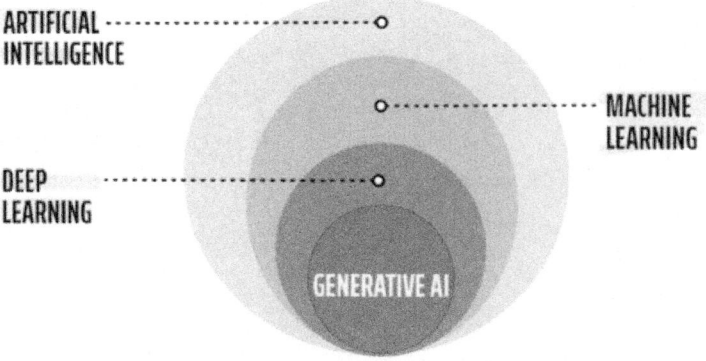

Figure 3: Hierarchy of Artificial Intelligence

Deep learning, a subfield within **machine learning**, plays a pivotal role in the evolution of generative AI. It is essential to recognize that deep learning is not a rival technology to machine learning but a constituent subfield that has significantly contributed to its advancement. The power of deep learning becomes particularly evident when dealing with vast amounts of data, where it consistently demonstrates superior performance.

The scope of deep learning extends beyond numerical data, encompassing various modalities such as text, images, and sounds. Although the conceptualization of deep learning dates back considerably, the absence of technologies capable of translating theory into practice hindered its realization into practical applications. This gap persisted until the advent of hardware advancements, prominently GPU technology, coupled with the emergence of software frameworks like **TensorFlow** and **Keras**, which greatly facilitated the transformation of deep learning theories into practical implementations.

The synergy of hardware improvements, the abundance of available data, and the development of sophisticated software tools has ushered in a new era for deep learning. This transformation has paved the way for the creation of tools such as **ChatGPT** and **DALL-E**, which have simplified our lives and become integral components in various applications.

The advent of transformer architecture marked a pivotal moment in the landscape of deep learning, allowing for a significant leap forward in various modalities such as text, images, and sounds. While rooted in history, the conceptualization of deep learning faced practical implementation challenges until recent advancements addressed these obstacles. The breakthrough came with the convergence of transformative technologies, notably **GPU** acceleration, and the development of comprehensive software frameworks like **TensorFlow** and **Keras**.

This synergy of hardware improvements and abundant available data set the stage for a transformative era in deep learning. The result has been the creation of powerful tools such as ChatGPT and DALL-E, which simplify our daily lives and become integral components in diverse applications. The journey from the conceptualization of deep learning to the realization of practical tools underscores the profound impact of the transformer's architecture and its role in shaping the trajectory of artificial intelligence.

Behind the scenes of these groundbreaking tools lies the paradigm of **Generative AI**. The ability of Generative AI to create content that goes beyond the mere replication of existing data sets it apart. The advancements in generative models have been made possible by the continuous evolution of deep learning principles, leveraging the enhanced capabilities provided by modern hardware and software ecosystems.

The journey from **deep learning** theories to practical applications, facilitated by technological innovations, has significantly shaped the landscape of artificial intelligence. The emergence of powerful tools like **ChatGPT** and **DALL-E** showcases the potential of **Generative AI**, which is revolutionizing how we interact with and generate content in the digital realm. The ongoing progress in this field promises further advancements, making **Generative AI** a focal point in the current and future artificial intelligence trends.

In the rapidly evolving field of artificial intelligence, generative AI has emerged as a significant subfield, encompassing a range of models reshaping the landscape of technology and innovation. **Gartner**, a renowned authority in technological research and analysis, has comprehensively categorized this domain, as illustrated in Figure 4. The foundation of this categorization lies in the concept of Foundation Models, which serve as the bedrock of the generative AI arena.

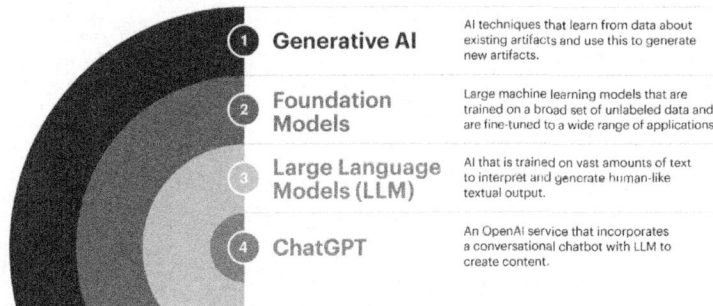

Figure 4: Hierarchy of Artificial Intelligence
Source: Gartner (2023)

These **foundational models** are pivotal in understanding the subsequent development of **Large Language Models** (LLMs), representing a more specialized and advanced subset within the generative AI field. LLMs, characterized by their expansive datasets and sophisticated algorithms, have been instrumental in advancing the capabilities of AI in understanding and generating human language. This significant progression underlines the evolution from general AI foundations to more complex and nuanced applications (Yang et al., 2023; Moor et al., 2023; Zhou et al., 2023; Qin et al., 2023).

Bommasani et al. (2021) conducted a study that observed that after the adaptation of the foundation model, it can successfully perform a wide range of tasks. Through this adaptation, the model has demonstrated effective performance in tasks such as question answering, sentiment analysis, information extraction, image captioning, object recognition, and instruction following. Specifically, the model has shown the ability to generate accurate and meaningful answers in question-answering tasks, detect emotional tones in sentiment analysis, extract crucial information in information extraction tasks, produce descriptive expressions effectively in image captioning tasks, identify objects accurately in object recognition tasks, and proficiently execute instructions in instruction following tasks. This adaptation enhances the foundation model's versatility and capability to accomplish multiple tasks, allowing for its effective utilization in various application domains (Figure 5).

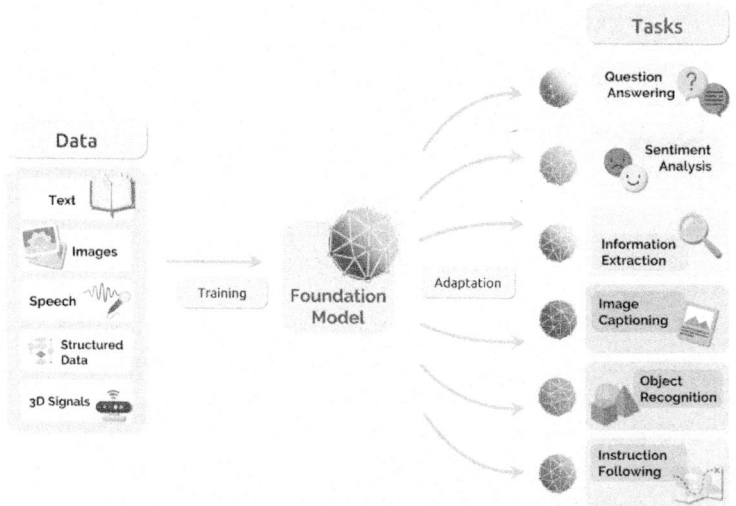

Figure 5: The wide range of tasks of the foundation model.
Source: Bommasani, R., Hudson, D. A., Adeli, E., Altman, R., Arora, S., von Arx, S., ... & Liang, P. (2021)

According to Yang's recent study (2023), the foundational models employed for decision-making undergo a comprehensive process. Initially trained on extensive and diverse datasets, these foundation models serve as versatile knowledge repositories (Figure 6). The adaptation process involves tailoring these models for specific tasks by engaging with external entities and incorporating valuable feedback. This dynamic interaction enhances the models' capabilities and decision-making efficacy across a spectrum of applications. Yang's research underscores the significance of this adaptive approach in optimizing the utility of foundation models in real-world decision-making scenarios and fostering continuous improvement.

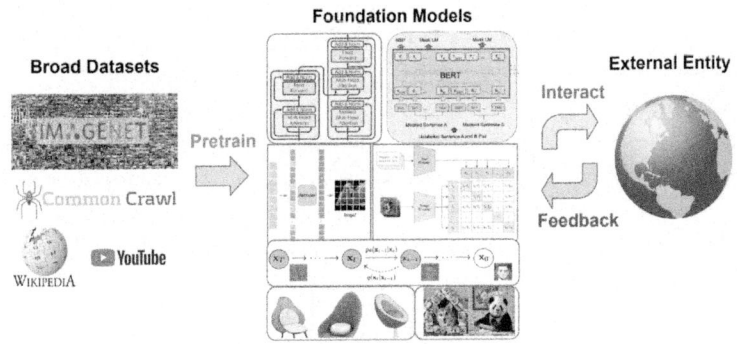

Figure 6: Foundation Models
Source: Yang, S., Nachum, O., Du, Y., Wei, J., Abbeel, P., & Schuurmans, D. (2023)

A paramount example of this advancement is ChatGPT, a model that Gartner places as a further progression in LLMs. ChatGPT, with its nuanced language processing and generation abilities, epitomizes the culmination of years of research and development in the field. Its ability to engage in coherent and contextually relevant dialogues marks a significant milestone in AI's journey towards mimicking human-like interactions.

Generative modeling, a branch of machine learning, focuses on training models to generate new data that closely resembles a specific dataset. This approach is pivotal in advancing machine learning applications, as highlighted in Foster (2019).

There are several learning paradigms in artificial intelligence, each with distinct methodologies (Figure 7). **Supervised Learning** involves training algorithms on labeled datasets, where input data is paired with corresponding output labels, similar to a teacher guiding the learning process through labeled examples. **Unsupervised Learning**, in contrast, deals with unlabeled data, exploring inherent patterns without predefined output labels through techniques like clustering and dimensionality reduction. **Reinforcement Learning** draws inspiration from behavioral psychology, where an agent interacts with an environment, learning to make decisions through trial and error and receiving feedback through rewards or penalties. **Generative AI**, gaining recent prominence, focuses on creating new, synthetic data, diverging from traditional AI by generating novel outputs. Models like GPT showcase unprecedented capabilities in crafting realistic text and images. Each paradigm addresses unique aspects of Learning, collectively contributing to the multifaceted landscape of artificial intelligence.

Andrew Ng, a prominent figure in Deep Learning, predicts significant advancements in Generative AI and Supervised Learning, particularly in the next three years. This forecast is part of his widely recognized "**Generative AI for Everyone**" course in 2023, where he explores the learning paradigms in Artificial Intelligence. Ng, known for his expertise and influence in AI, anticipates substantial progress in these domains, emphasizing the potential for noteworthy developments and breakthroughs in the coming years.

However, it is worth noting that Ng does not express similar expectations for Reinforcement Learning and Unsupervised Learning. While he anticipates significant strides in Generative AI and Supervised Learning, his projections for the advancements in Reinforcement Learning and Unsupervised Learning appear to be more reserved within the same timeframe.

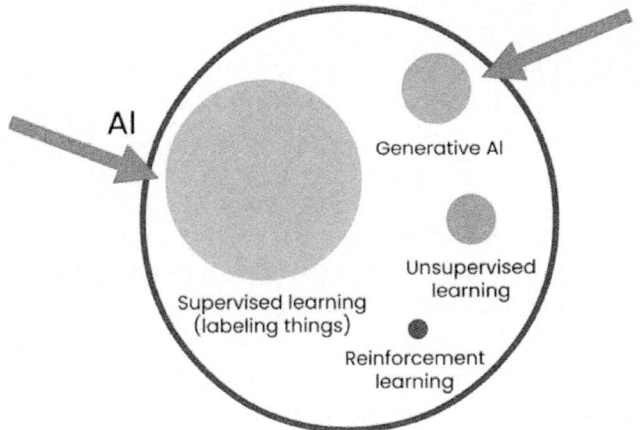

Figure 7: Learning Paradigms In Artificial Intelligence
Source: Deep Learning.AI. (2023). Generative AI for Everyone

Generative AI has surged in popularity due to its ability to foster creativity, fuel innovation, and tackle problems that demand imagination and ingenuity. Applications span from art and content creation to scientific research, showcasing the transformative potential of AI systems that go beyond prediction and classification to generate new and valuable content actively. As technological advancements continue, Generative AI stands at the forefront, captivating imaginations and reshaping the possibilities of artificial intelligence.

1.1.3 What is Generative AI?

Generative AI, or **GenAI**, is a type of Artificial Intelligence that learns from existing content through training, creating a statistical model. Generative AI uses this model to predict and generate new content when given a relevant prompt, showcasing its capacity for creative output within AI.

Generative AI is like a **magical wizard** in the world of Artificial Intelligence, creating all kinds of data like pictures, videos, sound, writing, and 3D models. It works by learning from existing data and then using that knowledge to make brand-new and unique things. What makes GenAI special is how good it is at making things that look real and are detailed, almost like a person could have made them. GenAI is worthwhile in many areas, like games, entertainment, and designing products.

This image has been generated with DALL-E using appropriate prompts

Generative models boast a rich history in artificial intelligence, tracing their roots back to the 1950s with the emergence of **Hidden Markov Models** (HMMs) and **Gaussian Mixture Models** (GMMs). Initially geared towards generating sequential data like speech and time series, the revolutionary era of Deep Learning catapulted generative models into a new realm of unprecedented performance enhancements, reshaping the landscape of AI innovation (Cao et al., 2023).

Recent improvements in machine learning, driven by abundant data and increased computing power, have brought about a new era in artificial intelligence, particularly in natural language processing (**NLP**). This progress is evident in advanced techniques like neural networks and transformers, significantly enhancing AI's ability to understand, interpret, and generate human language. Notably, these advancements have led to breakthroughs like question answering and natural language generation, showcasing unprecedented performance. While these developments offer exciting possibilities across various sectors, they raise critical ethical considerations like data privacy and AI bias. Therefore, responsible and ethical governance is essential for carefully deploying these technologies (Henrickson & Meroño-Peñuela, 2023).

Models like **ChatGPT**, **DALL**-E, and **Midjourney** have gained significant attention, prompting many individuals to delve deeper into their inner workings and uncover the secrets behind their impressive performance (Cao et al., 2023). Understanding these advanced language models, especially **ChatGPT**, is now a focus for researchers and enthusiasts. There is a growing interest in grasping the underlying principles and innovations that make these models stand out in natural language processing. This curiosity reflects technological advancements and hints at their potential applications and challenges in various fields.

The roots of generative AI trace back to significant milestones in the mid-2000s with the introduction of technologies like Google Translate in 2006 and the launch of Siri in 2011. These early instances showcased the potential of AI in generating content, from translations to voice-activated assistants on our devices and predicting our following words while typing or suggesting search queries.

Generative AI encompasses AI systems constructed on foundation models, possessing capabilities beyond those of earlier AI, particularly in content generation. Although capable of non-generative functions like sentiment classification based on call transcripts, these foundation models demonstrate substantial advancements compared to their predecessors. For the sake of simplicity in this article, the term "**Generative AI**" encompasses all use cases involving foundation models (Chui et al., 2023).

However, the turning point that brought Generative AI into the global spotlight occurred in 2023 when "OpenAI announced GPT-4, claiming it could outperform 90% of humans on the SAT." This proclamation marked a significant leap forward in the capabilities of generative models. The landscape shifted as this announcement showcased the potential of AI systems to understand and replicate language and excel at complex tasks traditionally associated with human intelligence.

The rising popularity of generative AI is due to fast-paced technological advancements. Notably, the emergence of ChatGPT, which reached a staggering milestone of 100 million users in just two months, surpassed the adoption rates of tech giants like Google Translate and Instagram (Figure 8). This unprecedented speed in user adoption underscores the growing significance of generative AI in reshaping how we interact with and leverage artificial intelligence in various aspects of our lives (Hu, 2023).

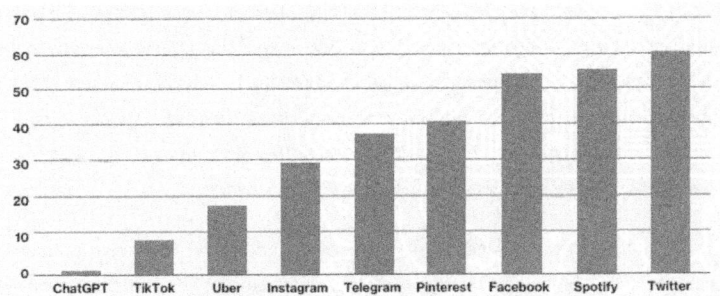

Figure 8: Generative AI's Popularity Growth
Source: MIT Technology Review Insights (2023)

While generative AI is not a recent invention, the convergence of breakthroughs in technology, ambitious claims by significant players like OpenAI, and the swift adoption of advanced models like GPT-4 have propelled Generative AI into the forefront of global discourse, marking a new era in artificial intelligence and its applications across diverse domains.

Gen AI offers the skills to create art, generate code, or write poems, leading to revolutionary changes in various industries (Baidoo-Anu & Ansah, 2023; Mannuru et al., 2023). This technology is built on a structure called foundation models, commonly known as machine learning models. Previous machine learning models were akin to preparing a specific French dish, meticulously crafted for a singular culinary task, like translating a classic bouillabaisse recipe. In contrast, Gen AI emerges as a gourmet chef, capable of translating recipes and conjuring entirely novel culinary creations based on the provided instructions.

Generative AI is a remarkable branch of artificial intelligence, showcasing its ability to craft diverse forms of content ranging from text, imagery, and audio to synthetic data (Mannuru et al., 2023). Operating within the broader framework of Deep Learning, Generative AI harnesses the power of artificial neural networks, demonstrating its versatility in handling labeled and unlabeled data through various methods, including supervised, unsupervised, and semi-supervised approaches.

Gen AI's domain is not limited to creative content; it can offer innovative solutions in various sectors, from simple tasks to writing customized captions for pictures and even more complex tasks, such as designing effective drug molecules (Levy & Rector-Brooks, 2023).

The basic models emerged with the transformer neural network architecture introduced in 2017. This architecture has transformed artificial intelligence into what can be likened to a magician's toolkit. Just like a skilled magician who effortlessly adapts to various tricks, this technology requires no manual data preparation and, through extensive pre-training, enables models to adjust to a diverse array of generalized tasks seamlessly.

This adaptability and its user-friendly nature are among the hallmarks of Gen AI. As Gen AI becomes increasingly accessible to more and more people, its potential to transform everyday lives in many areas, from education to health, climate change, and the challenges beyond, is increasing. With advanced technology and creative solutions, Gen AI can shape the future by solving problems worldwide (Ausat et al., 2023; Biswas, 2023a; Biswas, 2023b; Agathokleous et al., 2023).

Recent improvements in GenAI, like GPT (Generative Pre-trained Transformer) and Midjourney, have made it even better. These improvements show how GenAI is improving with technology and can do even more cool stuff. GenAI's improved abilities open new opportunities to solve tricky problems, make art, and help with science.

As GenAI keeps improving, we are entering a time when it can be a helpful tool for many different jobs. It is like a creative tool that can change how things work in different industries, improving them and helping with new ideas.

Generative language models and generative image models exemplify the fascinating capabilities of machine learning. In the realm of language, generative language models undergo a training process where they meticulously analyze patterns within language from a vast dataset. This training empowers them to predict the following elements in a given text. Essentially, these models learn to understand and replicate the nuances of language, enabling them to generate coherent and contextually relevant content based on the patterns they have discerned.

On the visual front, generative image models operate using innovative techniques like diffusion. When given a prompt or related imagery, these models showcase their transformative prowess by converting random noise into images or generating new images based on the provided prompts. This process highlights the dynamic nature of generative image models, demonstrating their ability to bring forth novel visual content through a blend of learned techniques and creative interpretation.

Both generative language and image models are remarkable examples of how machine learning can understand and create content in language and visual art through training and innovative methodologies. These models represent a convergence of technological ingenuity and creative potential, opening new avenues for generating diverse and contextually rich outputs (Cao et al., 2023).

Generative AI, exemplified by models like ChatGPT, presents many promising applications across diverse industries, encompassing business, education, healthcare, and content generation. *Generative AI could revolutionize customer interactions, automate routine tasks, and enhance decision-making processes in the business sector. Educational institutions may benefit from their ability to create interactive learning materials and provide personalized tutoring* (Lim et al., 2023).

Generative AI might contribute to medical research, aid in diagnostics, and streamline administrative tasks in healthcare. Furthermore, its proficiency in content generation holds implications for creative industries, journalism, and marketing, promising innovative and efficient approaches to content creation. The versatility of Generative AI positions it as a transformative force with the potential to reshape conventional practices and bring about substantial advancements across various domains (Fui-Hoon Nah et al., 2023).

"Generative AI is the next frontier in AI, with the potential to revolutionize the way we create and interact with content. It has the potential to create new forms of art, music, and literature, and to revolutionize the way we design products and services."

Andrew Ng
Founder of DeepLearning.AI

1.2. DISCRIMINATIVE AND GENERATIVE TECHNIQUE

To comprehend the nuances of **Generative AI**, it is essential to delve into the broader landscape of machine learning models and explore the distinction between generative and discriminative techniques. In this context, discriminative models play a crucial role. These models are specifically designed to classify or predict labels for given data points. During their training phase, discriminative models extensively utilize labeled datasets, allowing them to discern intricate relationships between the features of data points and their associated labels. Consequently, discriminative models become proficient at predicting labels for new, unseen data points after training. Now, let us explore how generative models differ in their approach and application.

In machine learning models, intense learning, a fundamental categorization emerges: generative and discriminative models. Discriminative models, dedicated to classifying or predicting labels for data points, undergo training with a labeled dataset. These models decipher the intricate relationship between data point features and their corresponding labels, empowering them to predict labels for new data points post-training.

This image has been generated with DALL-E using appropriate prompts

On the other hand, generative models set themselves apart by creating novel data instances based on a learned probability distribution from existing data. The intrinsic capability of generative models lies in their aptitude to generate entirely new content, providing a creative and exploratory dimension to artificial intelligence. Thus, within the dynamic landscape of AI, Generative AI emerges as a fascinating intersection of technology and creativity, ushering in a new era of innovative content creation and data synthesis.

In artificial intelligence, particularly machine learning, understanding the distinction between generative and discriminative models is crucial, and it hinges on the concepts of 'generate' and 'classify.' Discriminative models excel in classification, learning to differentiate between categories by focusing on decision boundaries and directly modeling the conditional probability P(Y|X). In contrast, generative models are creators who learn data distribution, aiming to generate new data points that mimic the original dataset. They do this by understanding the joint probability P(X, Y), encompassing a broader data distribution perspective. Discriminative models are best suited for tasks requiring precise classification, while generative models generate data and provide insights into the underlying data structure. This highlights the wide range of applications and implications of these foundational AI model types.

In machine learning and deep learning, models are broadly categorized into generative and discriminative, as highlighted in **Google Cloud Tech**'s educational video "**Introduction to Generative AI**" This distinction is crucial in understanding the functionalities and applications of these models in various contexts.

Discriminative models are designed primarily for classification tasks. They are trained on labeled datasets and learn the relationship between the features of the data points (inputs) and their corresponding labels (outputs). The primary function of a discriminative model is to predict labels for new data points based on this learned relationship. Essentially, these models learn and utilize the conditional probability distribution, or P(Y|X) - the probability of the output (Y) given the input (X).

For instance, in identifying whether an image depicts a dog or a cat, the discriminative model focuses on classifying the image based on learned features associated with each category (Figure 9).

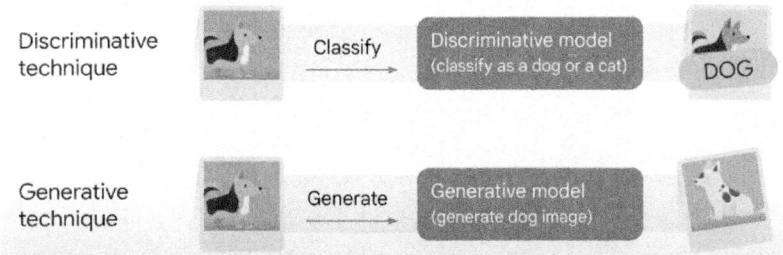

Figure 9: Learning Techniques
Source: Stripling, G. (2023)

In contrast, generative models are adept at creating new data instances. They do this by learning the probability distribution of the existing data and generating new content that aligns with this learned distribution. Generative models capture the joint probability distribution, or P(X, Y) - the probability of both the data and the labels. This enables them to predict and generate new instances, such as producing a new image of a dog, by understanding what characterizes such an image. The generative model's capacity to generate new content makes it distinct and versatile.

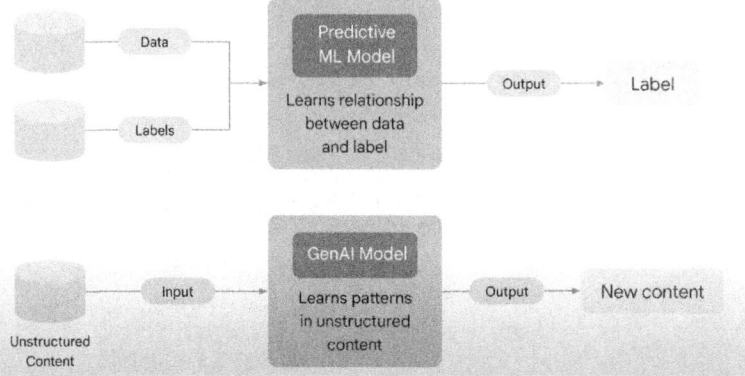

Figure 10: Traditional Machine Learning Model and Generative AI Model Difference
Source: Stripling, G. (2023)

The video encapsulates this difference with illustrative examples. While a traditional machine learning model (discriminative) focuses on learning the relationship between data and a label to predict an output, a generative AI model learns patterns in content to create new content (Figure 10). A key distinguishing factor is the nature of the output: generative AI typically does not produce outputs that are mere numbers, classes, or probabilities (like spam or not spam) but instead generates new, original data instances.

This distinction between generative and discriminative models, as presented by Google Cloud Tech, provides an essential understanding of the capabilities and applications of these two fundamental types of machine learning models.

CHAPTER 2
DIVERSE CAPABILITIES OF GENERATIVE AI

2.1 NAVIGATING GENERATIVE AI'S DIVERSE CAPABILITIES

Generative AI is ushering in a transformative era, significantly shaping the landscape of knowledge work. While earlier iterations of automation technology primarily targeted data-centric tasks, the distinctive cognitive capabilities of generative AI propel its influence beyond the confines of traditional automation. This shift is particularly pronounced in knowledge work, where decision-making and collaborative activities, previously considered less amenable to automation, now stand at the forefront of AI impact.

The essence of generative AI lies in its natural language proficiency, allowing it to engage with complex cognitive tasks. Unlike its predecessors, which excelled in automating data management, generative AI's potential extends into areas that demand nuanced thinking and human-like understanding. McKinsey's recent insights underscore this paradigm shift, highlighting a substantial increase in the automation potential for tasks involving the application of expertise. The technical potential for automating expertise applications has witnessed a remarkable 34-percentage-point surge.

Furthermore, once deemed less susceptible to automation, management and talent development have experienced a noteworthy transformation. The automation potential for these functions has surged **from 16 percent in 2017 to a robust 49 percent in 2023**, signaling a significant evolution in how generative AI can augment and streamline knowledge work. This trajectory underscores the profound impact that generative AI is set to exert on the intricate dynamics of decision-making, collaboration, and the application of expertise in the contemporary knowledge work landscape (Figure 11).

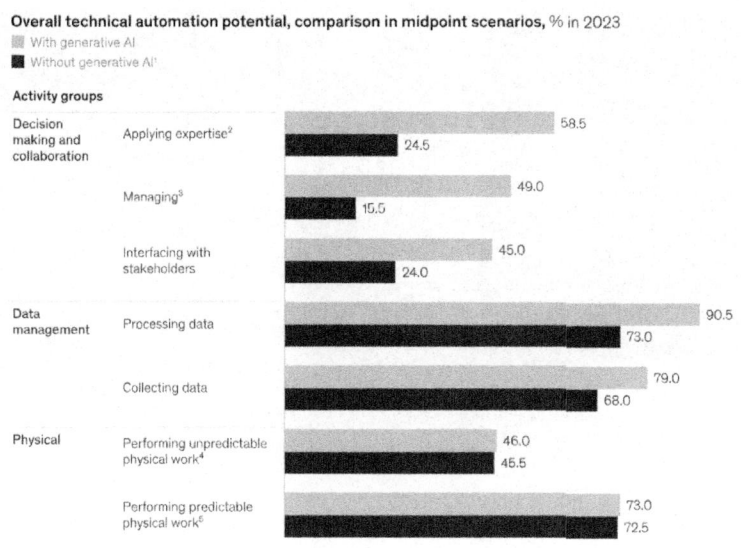

Figure 11.: Generative AI's impact on collaboration and the application of expertise
Source: McKinsey (2023)

Large Language Models (LLMs) have demonstrated various capabilities, as illustrated in Figure 12. Among these, Modular Arithmetic, Debugging, and Comprehension proficiency stand out. These models have showcased their ability to excel in areas beyond traditional language-related tasks, such as problem-solving in Modular Arithmetic, aiding in debugging code, and enhancing comprehension of complex information. It is important to note that these examples are just a glimpse of LLMs' diverse and expanding horizons as they continue to evolve and adapt to various challenges and domains.

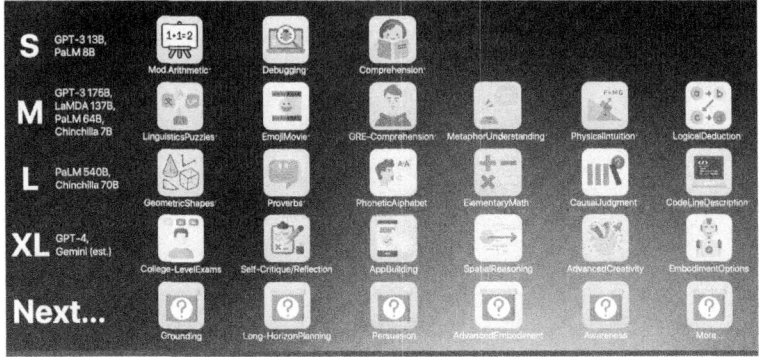

Figure 12: Emerging Abilities of Large Language Models
Source: LifeArchitect (2023)

Modular Arithmetic Proficiency:

- LLMs exhibit a notable achievement in mastering modular arithmetic, showcasing their capability to perform computations within modular number systems. This proficiency extends their utility to mathematical problem-solving and computational tasks that involve modular operations.

Debugging Skills:

- LLMs have demonstrated remarkable debugging skills, allowing them to identify and rectify errors within code or textual content. This emergent ability positions LLMs as valuable tools in software development, content editing, and quality assurance processes.

Enhanced Comprehension:

- The evolving capabilities of LLMs include enhanced comprehension, enabling them to grasp complex contexts and nuances within diverse inputs. This advancement in comprehension contributes to more accurate and contextually relevant outputs, making LLMs versatile in various language-related applications.

The expectations and prospects in this domain are visually depicted in Figure 12, presenting a roadmap for the evolving capabilities of LLMs. As these models continue to unlock new achievements, the landscape of their applications is expected to expand, offering solutions to an increasingly diverse set of challenges.

McKinsey's recent insights emphasize that advances in technical capabilities are poised to have the most significant impact on activities performed by educators, professionals, and creatives. This aligns with the overarching theme that Generative AI, with its proficiency in natural language understanding, is reshaping the landscape of knowledge work. The transformative potential extends to diverse sectors, and its profound influence is particularly noteworthy in education and technology, where automation potential is undergoing a faster-than-expected evolution. The technical capabilities of Generative AI are becoming a driving force, ushering in a new era that reshapes the roles of educators, professionals, and creatives in profound ways (Figure 13).

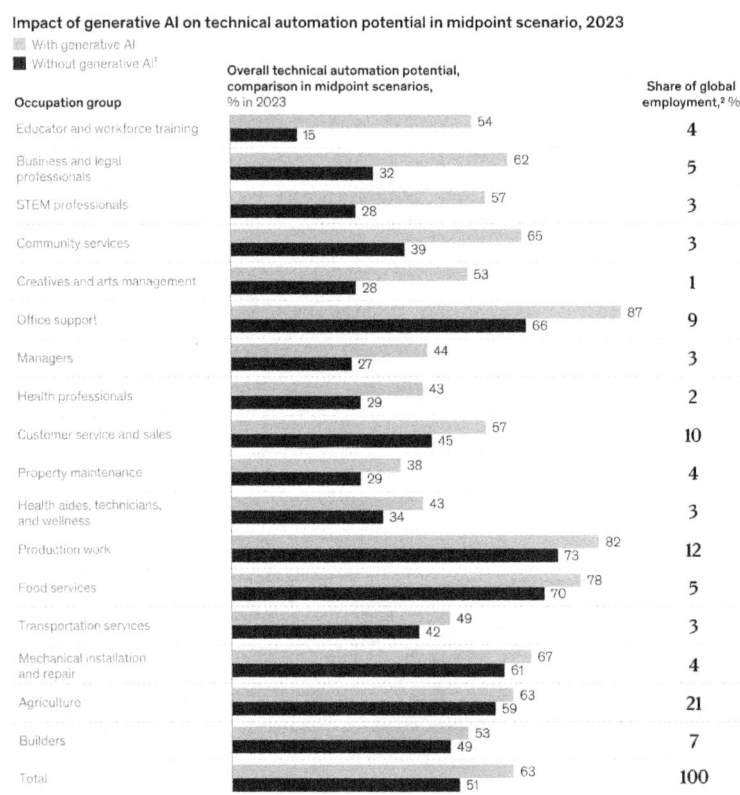

Figure 13: Impact of Generative AI on technical automation potential

Source: McKinsey (2023)

2.2.1 Writing, Reading And Chatting

Andrew Ng's "**Generative AI for Everyone**" course offered by DeepLearning.AI is a comprehensive exploration of Generative AI that unveils its remarkable aptitude, particularly in writing, reading, and chatting. The course delves into the intricacies of how Generative AI excels in crafting high-quality written content, displaying a nuanced understanding of context and style. It further emphasizes the technology's adeptness in comprehending and interpreting diverse written materials, showcasing its potential for applications ranging from content summarization to language translation.

In chatting, Generative AI emerges as a conversational virtuoso, navigating natural language interactions with a finesse that reflects advancements in language generation models. Andrew Ng's insights in the course meticulously unpack the underlying mechanisms that empower Generative AI to engage in meaningful and contextually relevant conversations, making it a pivotal tool in the evolution of conversational AI.

This detailed examination within the course highlights the current capabilities of Generative AI in these specific domains and hints at its future potential in shaping the landscape of written communication, content generation, and interactive dialogue. The course provides a profound understanding of how Generative AI is not just a technological marvel but a transformative force with far-reaching implications for diverse applications.

This image has been generated with DALL-E using appropriate prompts

Various powerful AI tools cater to diverse creative tasks, each possessing unique features. These tools, including **ChatGPT** for versatile language tasks, **Writesonic** for diverse copywriting needs, **Midjourney** facilitating art creation through text descriptions, and **Replit** supporting coding learning and application development, showcase the growing landscape of artificial intelligence applications. **Synthesia** enables the creation of speaking avatars for videos, while **Soundraw** generates music based on user-selected moods or activities. **Fliki** and **Starrytars** produce TikTok videos and avatars from user-provided ideas or descriptions. **Remini** enhances old or low-quality photos, **Pictory** is a comprehensive video editing tool, and **Wordtune** uses AI for text summarization. This dynamic AI toolbox reflects the evolving nature of artificial intelligence in creative domains. While maintaining their popularity, these AI tools will continue to become more widespread and increase their user base.

Today, transforming text into image or image into text signifies significant advances in computer science and artificial intelligence. The origins of these advances date back to the mid-20th century and the first steps of computers and artificial intelligence. Alan Turing's work on artificial intelligence in the 1950s (Turing, 1950) and the first artificial neural networks developed at MIT in the 1960s laid the foundation for today's technological advances.

In particular, Yan LeCun's work on Convolutional Neural Networks (CNN) with the MNIST data set revealed how successful artificial intelligence could be in visual perception. These studies took place in the late 1980s and early 1990s, heralding the Deep Learning revolution. Yan LeCun and his team successfully recognized handwritten digits, marking the beginning of a new era in AI's ability to process visual data (LeCun, 1998).

Today, Generative AI technologies can successfully perform more complex tasks, such as converting text to image or image to text. These advances were made possible by developing innovative AI models such as GANs (Generative Adversarial Networks). GANs were introduced by Ian Goodfellow and colleagues in 2014 and have revolutionized AI's ability to generate content (Goodfellow, 2014). Thanks to these technologies, AI is no longer limited to data analysis and classification but can also be used for creative and artistic work.

This historical perspective shows how Yan LeCun's work on the CNN and MNIST datasets plays a critical role in our understanding of the power and potential of Generative AI today. These groundbreaking technological advances allow AI to showcase its information processing and analytical capabilities and creativity and design capabilities. This critical milestone affects both the world of science and our daily lives.

According to McKinsey's recent survey responses, hiring tech talent has shown signs of becoming more manageable since 2022. The findings of an April 2023 survey further highlight a positive trend, specifically in the domain of generative AI, indicating that the challenge of finding talent in this field is already diminishing. The survey reveals a notable decrease in respondents reporting difficulties in organizations' hiring processes for AI-related roles. This positive shift is particularly evident in roles such as AI Data Scientists, Software Engineers, Data Engineers, Data Visualization Specialists, and Data Architects. The increasing ease in hiring for these positions signifies a positive trajectory in the availability and accessibility of skilled professionals in generative AI. As this trend continues, the progression is anticipated to lead to further facilitation of tasks and operations in various industries, enhancing overall efficiency in the foreseeable future (Figure 14).

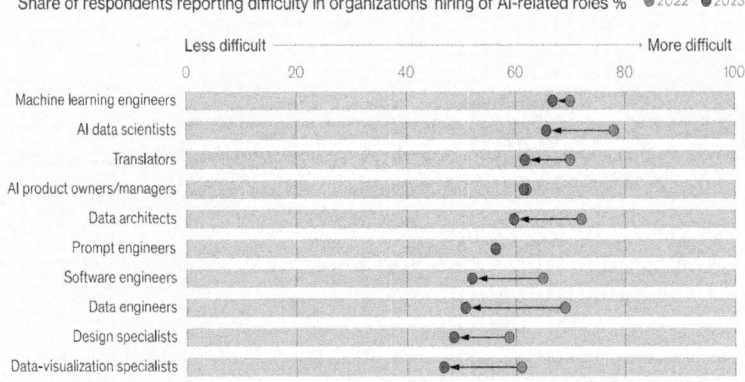

Figure 14: Hiring for AI-related roles
Source: MIT Technology Review Insights (2023)

2.2 DALL·E 2: A CREATIVE LEAP IN GENERATIVE AI

In this book, despite many different models, We would like to explain why we have dedicated a special place to DALL·E.

In the field of **NLP** (Natural Language Processing), there has been a long history of success in tasks related to text, such as sentiment analysis, summarization, and categorization, by detecting relationships between words through embeddings. Chat GPT represents the latest achievement in this field.

However, there is a different success story regarding computers understanding images. Yann LeCun's success in the early 1990s with Convolutional Neural Networks (CNNs) using the MNIST dataset (Figure 15), followed by similar success with the CIFAR dataset, marked the beginning in this domain. Subsequently, with ImageNet, pre-trained models, and later algorithms like YOLO, deep learning witnessed remarkable achievements.

Figure 15: MNIST Dataset

CNN, proficiently distinguishing between cats and dogs, has played a pivotal role in fostering significant advancements in this field with the emergence of **ImageNet** in subsequent years. It has laid the groundwork for substantial progress and spurred research efforts in this domain.

The ability of CNNs to automatically extract features from images and make fine-grained distinctions has contributed to a wide range of applications, including object detection, medical image analysis, and even self-driving cars.

Deep learning achieved remarkable milestones with the emergence of **ImageNet**, pre-trained models (transfer learning), and later breakthroughs like **YOLO** (Figure 16). Furthermore, in the early 2020s, **Diffusion Models** emerged as generative models, mastering data generation by reversing noise addition, revolutionizing the world of artificial intelligence with their remarkable ability to create high-quality images, often surpassing GANs, as exemplified by DALL-E 2 by OpenAI (O'Connor, 2022).

The synergy between these pioneering developments, ImageNet and Diffusion Models has significantly shaped the landscape of artificial intelligence. While ImageNet provided a robust benchmark for image classification tasks, it also facilitated the training of deep neural networks on a large scale, enabling the rapid development of various computer vision applications.

On the other hand, Diffusion Models ushered in a new era of generative AI, enhancing image generation and data synthesis in diverse domains such as natural language and audio. The complementary nature of these advancements continues to fuel innovation in AI research, promising a future filled with more groundbreaking achievements and applications.

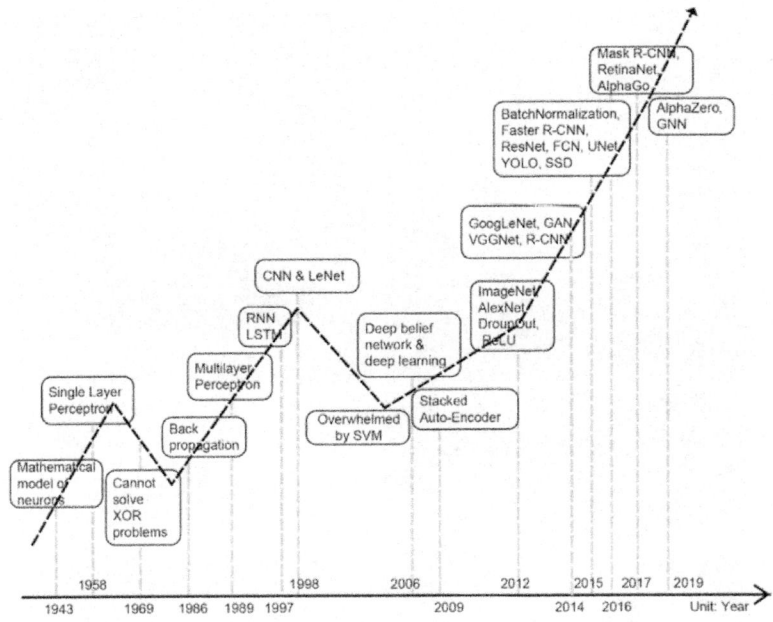

Figure 16: The Evolution of the Convolutional Neural Networks Architecture
Source: Cai, X. (2021)

Nevertheless, what DALL·E has brought is genuinely revolutionary. Therefore, we wanted to dedicate a section in this book to it. DALL·E can generate and interpret images using text inputs, revolutionizing image and text synthesis. In this book, we see an opportunity to understand and share the innovation and potential that DALL·E offers.

Figure 17: Various images generated by DALL-E 2
Source: O'Connor (2022)

DALL·E 2, a pioneering text-to-image generation model, was introduced by OpenAI in April 2022, capturing widespread public attention for its remarkable capabilities (Figure 17-18). The model's standout feature is its ability to create realistic images based on concise written prompts. Trained on an extensive dataset containing billions of text-image pairs gathered from the internet, DALL·E 2 has acquired diverse representations. Leveraging these representations intelligently, the model generates novel images, surpassing the variability encountered in the training data (Conwell & Ullman, 2022; Marcus et al. 2022; Kapelyukh et al., 2023; Leivada et al., 2023).

Figure 18: Selected 1024 × 1024 samples from a production version of Dall E model.
Source: Ramesh, A., Dhariwal, P., Nichol, A., Chu, C., & Chen, M. (2022)

Let us talk about how DALL-E works. Imagine it as a magic artist who can create pictures from words. First, it learns about words and pictures together. Then, when you give it a description (text), it uses this knowledge to make a unique code for the image. This code is like a recipe for the computer to follow. The computer uses this recipe to create a new picture that matches the description. The cool part is that DALL-E freezes its knowledge while creating pictures, like a superhero freezing time, so it can use what it learned to make incredible images!

DALL-E is an artificial intelligence model developed by OpenAI that makes it possible to create images from text. The working principle of DALL-E is based on the ability to take a text description and create an image that matches that description. This ability is achieved by using a method called "Clip objective." Clip objective is a source function used in the training of DALL-E. This function determines how the images generated by DALL-E are evaluated against a given text description. It is used to make DALL-E produce images compatible with the given text descriptions. For example, consider the phrase "**A pink cloudy sunset**." In order to produce an image matching this phrase, DALL-E can use the Clip objective to match images with the text description. Clip objective acts as a guide that directs DALL-E to produce the desired results by combining text and images (Figure 19). Clip objective is essential for improving the text-to-picture capabilities of DALL-E and similar models and producing more accurate results (Ramesh et al., 2022).

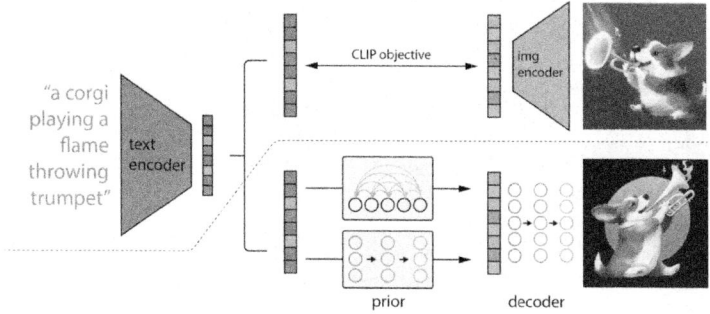

Figure 19: How DALL-E Works
Source: Ramesh, A., Dhariwal, P., Nichol, A., Chu, C., & Chen, M. (2022)

Cao et al. (2023) provide illustrative instances of AI-generated content in image generation. Specifically, they delve into the application of text instructions in guiding the OpenAI DALL-E-2 model. In this process, textual prompts are fed into the model, and as a response, the model generates two distinct images by the provided instructions. This exemplifies the model's capacity to translate textual input into visually coherent and contextually relevant images, showcasing the evolving capabilities of AI in the creative domain (Figure 20). The study sheds light on the potential of harnessing language instructions to influence the generation of diverse visual outputs, contributing to the ongoing discourse on the intersection of artificial intelligence and creative expression.

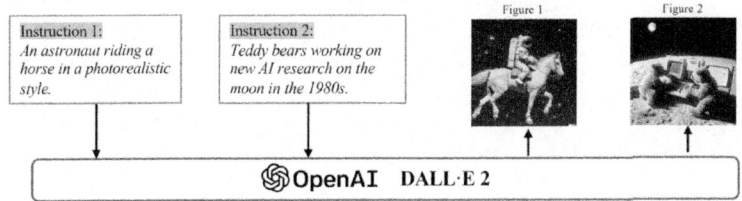

Figure 20: Examples of AI-generated content in image generation.
Source: Cao, Y., Li, S., Liu, Y., Yan, Z., Dai, Y., Yu, P. S., & Sun, L. (2023)

In recent years, a growing interest has been in developing generative models that can comprehend and create multimodal content. One particularly intriguing area of focus is vision-language generative models, designed to generate images from textual descriptions (**text-to-image**) or produce textual descriptions from images (**image-to-text**). These models find applications in diverse fields, including chatbots, image synthesis, and content creation for social media platforms (Figure 21) (Yasungaga, 2023).

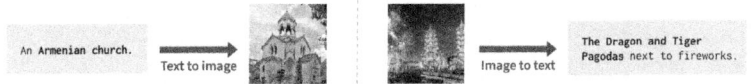

Figure 21: Text to image and image to text sample
Source: Yasungaga, M. (2023)

Notable advancements in text-to-image models comprise autoregressive Transformer-based approaches like DALL-E, CogView2, and Parti and diffusion-based models such as DALL-E 2, Stable Diffusion, Imagen, and Midjourney. Each image is represented as a sequence of visual tokens in the former category, and a Transformer is employed to generate images. Conversely, diffusion-based models create images using a diffusion model, with conditioning based on embedding input text. These developments mark significant progress in bridging the gap between textual and visual modalities and hold promise for many multimodal applications (Figure 22) (Yasungaga, 2023).

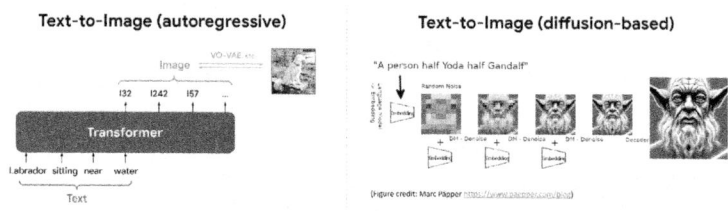

Figure 22: Text to image (autoregressive) and image to text sample (diffusion-based) Source:Yasungaga, M. (2023)

Cao et al. (2023) identified two main types of models: unimodal and multimodal. Unimodal models take instructions and produce content similarly, sticking to a single mode of operation (Figure 23). On the other hand, multimodal models are more versatile, handling instructions from one source and generating content in different ways. This classification helps us understand how models process information and generate outputs, highlighting the differences between straightforward unimodal systems and the more adaptable multimodal approaches.

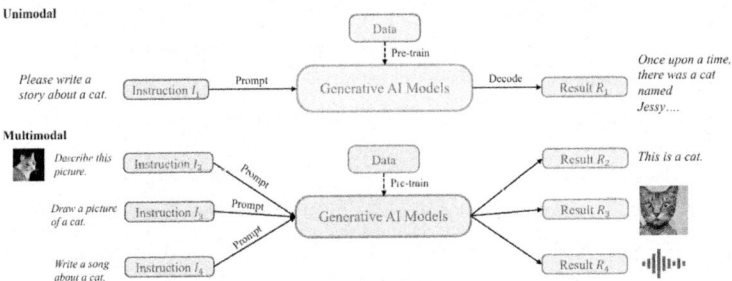

Figure 23 :Overview of Artificial Intelligence Generated Content
Source: Cao, Y., Li, S., Liu, Y., Yan, Z., Dai, Y., Yu, P. S., & Sun, L. (2023)

Even if we are not quite reaching the pinnacle of true artistic mastery, the advent of AI technologies enables us to access artistic creations that once demanded days of a genuine artist's dedication, all within seconds. Going beyond the constraints of limited datasets like **PASCAL VOC** and **COCO**, we are now equipped to identify objects with extensive datasets. These promising applications extend far beyond the realms of traditional artistic endeavors.

This transformative era is about accelerating artistic production and leveraging AI capabilities for the betterment of humanity. We are on the cusp of a revolution where AI, harnessed for various purposes, holds the potential to address crucial global issues. From the deployment of autonomous vehicles that redefine transportation to initiatives aimed at eliminating barriers for individuals with disabilities, the scope of applications is vast.

One of the remarkable facets of this revolution lies in utilizing AI to streamline daily life, making it more efficient and cost-effective. AI is contributing to a more seamless and resource-efficient existence through innovations in fields such as predictive maintenance, energy optimization, and infrastructure management.

To succeed in this profound transformation, embracing and adapting to advancements rather than resisting change Is crucial. It necessitates a proactive stance, a commitment to staying abreast of developments, and an eagerness to integrate these changes swiftly. As we witness this revolution unfold, the onus is on us to be on the side that actively embraces progress, driving positive change for the benefit of all. This is not merely a technological evolution but a testament to our collective ability to innovate and shape a future that promises a more accessible, efficient, and harmonious world for everyone.

"Like with all technological revolutions, I expect there to be significant impact on jobs, but exactly what that impact looks like is very difficult to predict...I believe that there will be far greater jobs on the other side of this, and that the jobs of today will get better...I think it's important to understand and think about GPT-4 as a tool, not a creature, which is easy to get confused, and it's a tool that people have a great deal of control over and how they use it. And second, GPT-4 and other systems like it are good at doing tasks, not jobs."

Sam Altman
CEO of OpenAI

Various images generated by DALL-E 2

CHAPTER 3
LARGE LANGUAGE MODELS (LLMs)

3.1 EXPLORING LARGE LANGUAGE MODELS (LLMs)

Large Language Models (LLMs) are adept at deciphering complex patterns in language, enabling them to perform a diverse range of tasks. They can generate logical reasoning chains, solve intricate logic and math puzzles, and have significant applications in robotics. In robotics, LLMs can plan and execute tasks, synthesize policies, design reward functions, and adapt to user preferences by employing few-shot learning with contextually rich text prompts. Their operations are not just data-driven but highly semantic, focusing on understanding and interpreting the meaning and context of inputs and outputs. This versatility allows LLMs to transition seamlessly from abstract, text-based tasks to practical, real-world applications in various domains (Mirchandani et al., 2023).

LLMs (Large Language Models) are developed using extensive datasets and incorporate billions of parameters, leading to unparalleled complexity. Such sophistication necessitates regulatory oversight, which must consider the inherent challenges in ensuring interpretability, maintaining fairness, and mitigating unintended consequences (Meskó & Topol, 2023).

Recent years have seen remarkable advancements in natural language processing (NLP) due to the development of large language models like the Generative Pre-trained Transformer (GPT-3). These sophisticated models are trained on extensive text datasets, enabling them to generate text closely resembling human writing. They excel in various language-related tasks, such as producing contextually relevant text, accurately answering questions, and efficiently completing other language-based tasks. This high accuracy and versatility in language understanding and generation marks a significant milestone in NLP (Kasneci et al., 2023).

LLMs constitute a significant subset of artificial intelligence (AI) systems, known for their capacity to process and understand natural language. These models undergo training on extensive datasets comprising billions of words from diverse textual materials such as articles, books, and various internet-based contents. The core architecture of LLMs is based on neural networks, which employ deep learning techniques. This architectural framework is essential for representing the complex associative relationships among words in the text-based training data. The training methodology for LLMs is often multi-tiered and may incorporate different levels of human involvement. During this training phase, LLMs are exposed to the nuances of language use, learning how words interact and relate in various contexts. This understanding enables LLMs to apply these patterns in executing natural language processing tasks, demonstrating their ability to interpret and generate human-like text (Thirunavukarasu et al., 2023).

The proliferation of pre-trained large language models has prompted growing concerns regarding their potential impact on influencing, persuading, and, in extreme instances, manipulating user preferences (Liu et al., 2023b).

The quest for achieving language intelligence in machines, initiated with the Turing Test in the 1950s, has been an ongoing exploration. Language, a complex system of human expressions governed by grammatical rules, presents a formidable challenge for developing AI algorithms capable of understanding and generating it. Language modeling, a critical approach, has evolved from statistical to neural models over the past two decades, culminating in the recent introduction of pre-trained language models (PLMs). These PLMs, pre-trained on extensive corpora using Transformer models, exhibit robust capabilities across various natural language processing (NLP) tasks. Researchers have observed that scaling the model size enhances capacity and introduces unique abilities, such as in-context learning. Large language models (LLMs), characterized by significant parameter scales, have become a focal point in recent research, showcasing advancements in academia and industry. The emergence of ChatGPT, a powerful AI chatbot based on LLMs, has garnered widespread attention, marking a crucial milestone in the technical evolution of LLMs and signaling a transformative impact on the broader AI community (Zhao et al., 2023a).

Zhao et al. (2023a) provide a comprehensive overview of the evolutionary trajectory of language models with a focus on their evolving task-solving capacities. The journey initiates with statistical language models, initially employed to augment specific tasks like retrieval or speech-related functions. This early stage leverages predicted probabilities to optimize task-specific approaches. In the future, the paradigm changes thanks to neural language models. They focus on learning versatile representations, reducing the need for manual feature engineering.

A subsequent milestone in this progression involves pre-trained language models. This phase witnesses a pivotal transition towards the acquisition of context-aware representations. These representations are meticulously honed and optimized to align with the requirements of downstream tasks. The latest stride in this evolution showcases Large LLMs, which undergo augmentation by exploring scaling effects on their model capacity. This transformative step positions LLMs as versatile and general-purpose task solvers capable of tackling diverse challenges.

Summing up the evolutionary process, there is a notable expansion in the scope of tasks that language models can effectively address. Simultaneously, there is a marked enhancement in the overall performance levels attained by these models across an extensive spectrum of tasks. This nuanced evolution underscores language models' adaptability and increasing efficacy in navigating complex language-based applications.

Figure 24 illustrates the evolutionary trajectory of language models (LM) across four generations, focusing on their evolving task-solving capabilities. It is crucial to acknowledge that the temporal boundaries for each stage are approximate and are primarily aligned with the publication dates of pivotal studies characterizing each stage. In representing neural language models, we abbreviate two critical studies as NPLM ("A neural probabilistic language model") and NLPS ("Natural language processing (almost) from scratch"). Due to spatial limitations, not all representative studies are included in this illustration to maintain brevity.

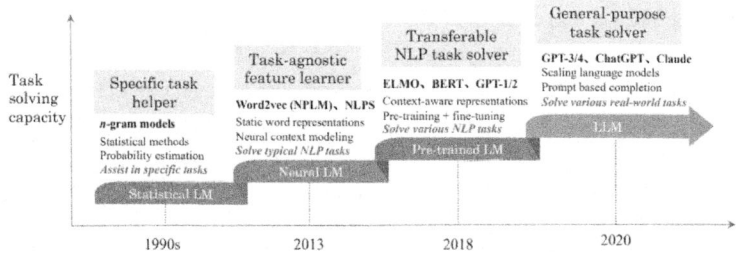

Figure 24: Evolutionary trajectory of language models (LM) across four generations
Source: Zhao, W. X., Zhou, K., Li, J., Tang, T., Wang, X., Hou, Y., ... & Wen, J. R. (2023a)

Below (Figure 25) is a chronological representation of large language models (with a size exceeding **10 billion parameters**) developed in recent years, with open-source models highlighted in yellow. This timeline provides a visual overview of the evolution and emergence of significant language models, showcasing the growth and contributions in the field.

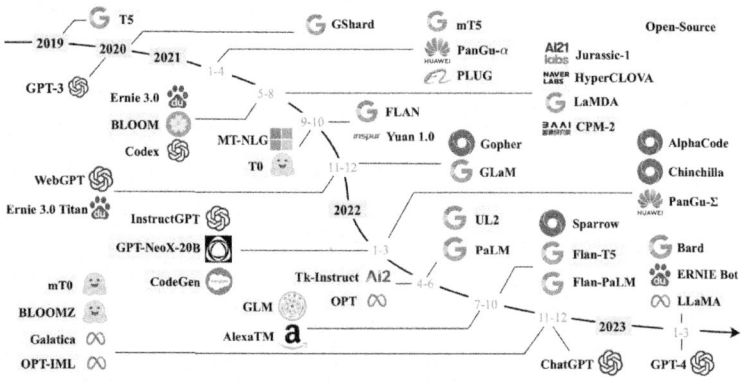

Figure 25: Chronological Representation Of Large Language Models
Source: Zhao, W. X., Zhou, K., Li, J., Tang, T., Wang, X., Hou, Y., ... & Wen, J. R. (2023a)

As depicted in Figure 26 of LifeArchitect's 2023-2024 analysis of Optimal Language Models, as of November 2023, GPT-4 is prominently featured in the forefront. This figure portrays GPT-4 as the current leader in the field, illustrating its superiority over other models in various aspects of performance and capability. The report also states that competition in the advanced language model field is expected to increase rapidly. This forecast suggests a rapidly evolving landscape where new advancements and contenders are expected to emerge, challenging GPT-4's current position of dominance.

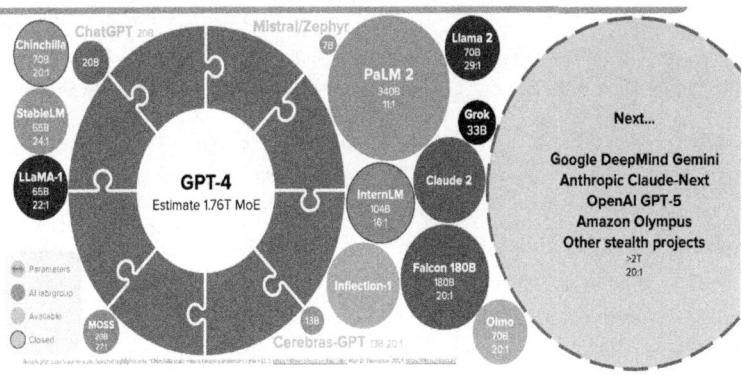

Figure 26: 2023-2024 analysis of Optimal Language Models
Source: LifeArchitect (2023)

The historical trajectory and capabilities of OpenAI's GPT are illustrated in Figure 27. This visual representation encapsulates the evolutionary journey of the GPT model, highlighting its various iterations, advancements, and expanding capabilities over time.

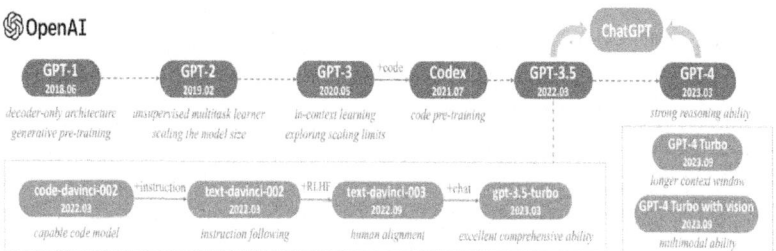

Figure 27: Historical Trajectory And Capabilities Of Openai's Gpt
Source: Zhao, W. X., Zhou, K., Li, J., Tang, T., Wang, X., Hou, Y., ... & Wen, J. R. (2023a)

LLMs are poised to significantly influence and enhance various critical domains, namely healthcare, finance, scientific research, law, and education, due to their advanced capabilities in handling complex tasks (Baidoo-Anu & Ansah, 2023; Biswas, 2023a; Biswas, 2023b). In healthcare, LLMs have demonstrated proficiency in tasks like medical information extraction, consultation, and mental health analysis, although concerns about misinformation and privacy remain. In education, LLMs show promise in assisting with learning and writing, enhancing student performance, and transforming teaching methodologies while posing challenges like plagiarism and bias. LLMs exhibit strong legal interpretation and reasoning skills in legal applications, aiding in legal document analysis and judgment prediction. However, they also raise issues related to legal ethics and confidentiality. In finance, LLMs are effective in various financial tasks like sentiment analysis and reasoning, but the risks of inaccurate information impacting financial markets call for careful monitoring. Lastly, LLMs assist across various stages in scientific research, from literature surveying to hypothesis generation and data analysis, offering substantial support in scientific writing and paper review. However, the accuracy and reliability of generated content need further enhancement. This multifaceted potential of LLMs across these domains highlights their transformative impact, albeit accompanied by challenges that need addressing to harness their capabilities thoroughly.

The recent advancements in LLMs have significantly impacted the research community and various domains, showcasing their versatility and enhanced capabilities. Regarding research directions, LLMs have evolved beyond classic scenarios to address new challenges and opportunities. Within subfields like classic Natural Language Processing (NLP) tasks, LLMs exhibit proficiency in word/sentence-level tasks, sequence tagging, information extraction, and text generation. LLMs also play a crucial role as Information Retrieval (IR) models, enhancing retrieval and recommendation systems. Integrating LLMs in multimodal contexts further expands their application, including vision-language alignment pre-training and evaluation methodologies (Figure 28).

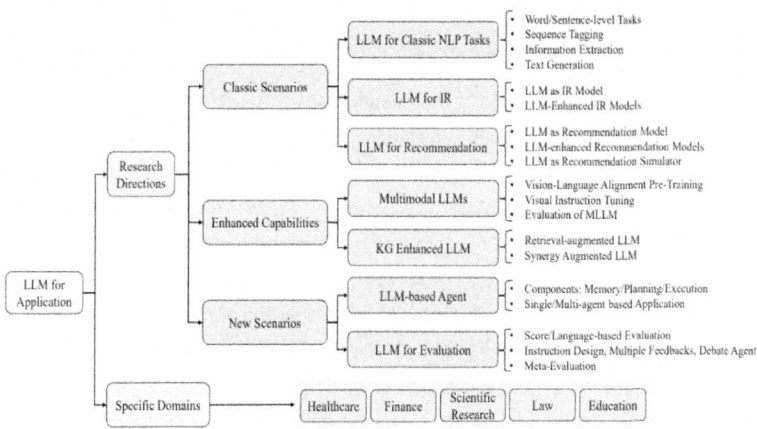

Figure 28: LLM for Application

Source: Zhao, W. X., Zhou, K., Li, J., Tang, T., Wang, X., Hou, Y., ... & Wen, J. R. (2023a)

Additionally, LLMs contribute to knowledge graph-enhanced models, retrieval-augmented LLMs, and synergy-augmented LLMs, incorporating components such as memory, planning, and execution. LLM-based agents are explored in single and multi-agent applications, demonstrating their adaptability. Furthermore, LLMs are utilized for evaluation purposes through score/language-based evaluation, instruction design, multiple feedback mechanisms, and debate agents, providing a comprehensive framework for meta-evaluation in diverse domains. Overall, the impact of LLMs extends across classic, enhanced, and emerging scenarios, influencing research trajectories and contributing to the evolution of various application domains (Zhao et al., 2023a).

LMs assign probabilities to sequences of words, aiming to identify the most likely word to occur next in a given context. This process involves leveraging statistical patterns learned during the model's training on extensive language datasets. By calculating the likelihood of various word sequences, LMs become proficient in predicting and generating coherent and contextually relevant text. The primary objective is to estimate the probability distribution of word occurrences. This enables the model to make informed predictions about the next word in a sequence based on the context provided.

Language models have a rich history dating back to the 1950s. The exploration of language modeling began with foundational approaches such as the Bag-of-Words model in the 1950s and 1960s, representing text as an unordered set of words without considering sequence or context. The N-gram model, also from the 1950s to 1960s, introduced the consideration of groups of N consecutive words to capture sequence information (Zhang & Zhou, 2010; Qader et al., 2019). Moving into the 1980s and 1990s, Hidden Markov Models (HMMs) depicted language as a sequence of hidden states and observable outputs, while the 1990s to 2010s saw the introduction of Recurrent Neural Networks (RNNs) and their extension, Long Short-Term Memory (LSTM) networks, which processed sequential data by maintaining internal states to capture context (Eddy, 2004; Rabiner & Juang, 1986). Fast forward to the 2010s, the Transformer architecture emerged, marking a significant milestone with its self-attention mechanism for processing variable length sequences (Wolf et al., 2020). This ongoing evolution showcases language models' continuous development and refinement over the years (Figure 29).

In recent years, there has been a remarkable surge in the scale and capabilities of language models, catapulting the field of natural language processing into uncharted territories. This explosion of innovation has not only expanded the boundaries of what is achievable but has also revolutionized how we comprehend and generate human-like language. The continuous evolution of these language models is actively shaping the landscape of natural language understanding, paving the way for groundbreaking developments that hold significant promise for the future. As we witness these transformative strides, it becomes evident that advancements in language models are propelling the field toward even greater heights, offering a glimpse into the exciting possibilities that lie ahead.

Language Model	Description	"Large"?	Emergence
Bag-of-Words Model	Represents text as a set of unordered words, without considering sequence or context	No	1950s-1960s
N-gram Model	Considers groups of N consecutive words to capture sequence	No	1950s-1960s
Hidden Markov Models (HMMs)	Represents language as a sequence of hidden states and observable outputs	No	1980s-1990s
Recurrent Neural Networks (RNNs)	Processes sequential data by maintaining an internal state, capturing context of previous inputs	No	1990s-2010s
Long Short-Term Memory (LSTM) Networks	Extension of RNNs that captures longer-term dependencies	No	2010s
Transformers	Neural network architecture that processes sequences of variable length using a self-attention mechanism	Yes	2017-Present

Figure 29: A Brief History of Large Language Models
Source: Databricks (2023)

LLM is a remarkable example of the incredible capabilities that can be achieved through training on massive datasets. To truly appreciate the scale of its training, consider this: while an average person might read around 700 books throughout their lifetime, ChatGPT underwent training using an astonishing dataset of up to a staggering 1 trillion tokens. To put this into perspective, this amount of data is equivalent to processing information from more than 10 million books. In other words, ChatGPT has ingested an immense wealth of textual information, making it an exceptionally knowledgeable language model capable of generating coherent and contextually relevant text across a wide range of topics and tasks.

This image has been generated with DALL-E using appropriate prompts

In addition to this immense capacity for data absorption, LLMs possess a unique trait that sets them apart from human memory. While individuals may eventually forget the content of books they have read over time, Language Models (LMs) can retain and recall knowledge persistently. This characteristic positions LLMs as not only vast information repositories but also powerful tools for information retrieval and generation.

LLMs introduce a paradigm shift by automating numerous tasks traditionally carried out by humans. This automation not only expedites processes but also opens up avenues for individuals to delve into accelerated innovation. With LLMs at the forefront, software development takes on a faster pace, allowing for quicker iteration and implementation of ideas. The democratization of AI through LLMs means that a broader user base can harness the power of artificial intelligence, unlocking more use cases across diverse domains.

The benefits extend beyond speed and accessibility; LLMs are vital in reducing development costs. Automating monotonous tasks alleviates the burden on human resources and contributes to more efficient and cost-effective development processes. This reduction in development costs translates into a tangible advantage for individuals and organizations, fostering a more streamlined and economically viable approach to innovation.

Ultimately, incorporating LLMs in various workflows accelerates the pace of innovation and enhances Return on Investment (ROI). As tasks become automated and development costs decrease, projects' overall efficiency and effectiveness increase. This positive impact on ROI underscores the transformative potential of LLMs for individuals seeking to optimize processes, drive innovation, and achieve tangible results in an increasingly automated and AI-driven landscape.

LLMs go beyond hype, revolutionizing every industry by transforming traditional approaches and fostering a paradigm shift in artificial intelligence. Their impact spans healthcare, finance, entertainment, and technology, offering unparalleled language understanding for enhanced decision-making, streamlined operations, and innovative applications. LLMs democratize access to advanced natural language processing, adapting to various tasks and challenging traditional norms, ensuring a lasting and profound shift in industry dynamics.

LLMs fall within the domain of Deep Learning, representing a specific subset. This subset, namely Large Language Models, converges with Generative AI, showcasing the intersection of advanced language-based artificial intelligence and the broader field of generative models.

LLMs represent a revolutionary approach in artificial intelligence, offering the flexibility to be pre-trained for general language understanding and then fine-tuned for specific applications. Comparing it to training a dog, the first pre-training phase of an LLM is similar to teaching a dog basic commands like "sit," "come," "down," and "stay." On the other hand, fine-tuning is comparable to refining the dog's skills for specialized roles like police work, guiding, or hunting. In language models, this fine-tuning process allows customization for particular tasks (Ewald, 2023).

The concept extends to LLMs, which undergo pre-training to address common language challenges such as text classification, question answering, document summarization, and text generation. This foundational training equips them with a broad understanding of language nuances and context. Subsequently, fine-tuning enables adapting these models to solve specific problems in diverse fields like retail, finance, and entertainment. This process involves training LLMs on relatively more minor datasets specific to each field, tailoring their capabilities to meet the unique demands of distinct industries.

Training and fine-tuning Large Language Models is similar to training a versatile dog, refining basic commands into specialized skills. This adaptability positions LLMs as powerful tools capable of addressing various language challenges across various domains through general pre-training and targeted fine-tuning.

LLMs distinguish themselves through three fundamental pillars, each contributing to their remarkable capabilities (Ewald, 2023):

1. **Large:**

    LMs leverage the power of scale in two crucial aspects. Firstly, they undergo training on extensive datasets, exposing them to various linguistic patterns and contexts. This extensive training dataset serves as the foundation, enabling the models to grasp the intricacies of language comprehensively. Secondly, LLMs boast many parameters, enhancing their capacity to capture and represent complex relationships within the data. This sheer scale sets them apart, allowing for a more nuanced understanding and generation of human-like text.

2. **General Purpose:**

    The generality of LLMs lies in their proficiency across diverse human languages. LLMs transcend language barriers and demonstrate adaptability to many linguistic structures by encapsulating commonalities among languages. Despite resource restrictions, they exhibit a remarkable ability to navigate the nuances of various languages. This general-purpose nature positions LLMs as versatile tools capable of addressing a wide range of language-related tasks, from translation to summarization, irrespective of the linguistic diversity they encounter.

3. **Pre-trained and Fine-tuned:**

    LLMs follow a two-fold process that begins with pre-training on a broad spectrum of language challenges using the aforementioned large dataset and parameter-rich architecture. This initial phase equips them with a foundational understanding of language. Subsequently, LLMs undergo fine-tuning, a process where they are adapted to specific tasks or domains using smaller, task-specific datasets. This dual-stage approach allows LLMs to strike a balance between a generalized understanding of language and task-specific expertise, making them adaptable to various applications across different fields.

The combination of scale, generality, and a two-phase training process renders Large Language Models unparalleled tools in natural language processing, showcasing their proficiency in understanding and generating text across diverse linguistic landscapes.

In the video "**What is generative AI and how does it work?**" by **Mirella Lapata**, she likely discussed that increasing the number of parameters in a Large Language Model enhances its functionality. This idea is based on the concept that having more parameters enables the model to learn complex patterns, relationships, and contextual details in the data it is trained on.

Researchers and practitioners have observed that as the scale of LLMs increases, their performance on various natural language processing tasks tends to improve. This is often called "**scaling laws**" in the context of neural networks (Figure 30). However, it is essential to note that there may be diminishing returns, and training huge models also comes with challenges, such as increased computational requirements and potential ethical considerations.

"**Scaling laws**" in neural networks describe the observed patterns as large language models (LLMs) increasing in size. Simply put, larger models perform better in natural language processing tasks, as shown in Figure 30. However, it is essential to consider diminishing returns, signifying that beyond a specific size, the added benefits diminish, and the resources needed for training and maintaining such models substantially increase. Challenges arise, particularly in computational requirements, as larger models demand more resources, making the training process resource-intensive. Additionally, ethical considerations are relevant due to the environmental impact of running massive computational processes for training these sizable models.

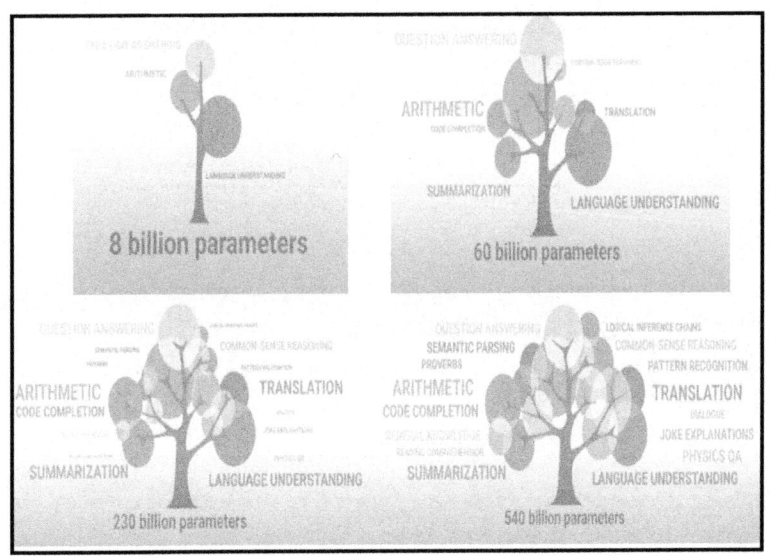

Figure 30: The scaling laws of LLMs
Source: Lapata, M. (2023)

3.2 BENEFITS AND RISKS OF USING LARGE LANGUAGE MODELS

Embarking on the journey to create large language models from scratch is undeniably daunting. It is essential to recognize that these endeavors demand significant investments in time and hardware resources. The initial phase involves collecting and cleaning extensive sets of textual data, a process crucial for the model's foundational understanding.

Access to a robust hardware infrastructure is imperative, necessitating ongoing computational power for the project's duration. Developing such models requires extensive research and engineering efforts involving the meticulous fine-tuning of deep learning algorithms and architectures through iterative processes. This iterative nature makes the entire endeavor time-consuming.

It is important to emphasize that these projects have substantial financial and human resource requirements. Moreover, considering the environmental impact of such resource-intensive processes is crucial for responsible development practices.

Creating large language models from scratch demands a collaborative, multidisciplinary approach. Overcoming the challenges mentioned above is critical to achieving successful outcomes. The complexity of this undertaking underscores the need for careful consideration of various factors, from data collection to hardware infrastructure, to ensure the responsible and effective development of large language models.

While creating a large language model (LLM) from scratch may pose challenges, leveraging LLMs developed by corporate entities offers a more straightforward solution. Now, let us delve into the various benefits that can be derived from using these established LLMs.

Utilizing LLMs offers many benefits, making them a powerful asset in natural language processing and artificial intelligence applications.

1. **Versatility Across Tasks:**

   One of the primary advantages of employing LLMs is their ability to serve multiple purposes. A single model can seamlessly adapt to various tasks, ranging from text classification and question answering to document summarization. This versatility streamlines the development process, as a unified model can be employed for a diverse set of language-related challenges.

2. **Efficient Fine-tuning Process:**

   The fine-tuning phase, a crucial step in tailoring models to specific tasks or domains, is notably streamlined with LLMs. These models require minimal field data for fine-tuning, allowing for a more efficient and resource-conscious adaptation to specialized applications. This efficiency accelerates the integration of LLMs into different industries, minimizing the data requirements for task-specific optimization.

3. **Continuous Performance Improvement:**

   LLMs exhibit a unique characteristic of continuous performance improvement as more data and parameters are introduced. With larger datasets and increased parameters, these models showcase an evolving proficiency in understanding and generating language. This adaptability ensures that LLMs stay at the forefront of language processing capabilities, providing enhanced performance as they encounter a broader range of linguistic nuances and complexities

4. Advanced Contextual Comprehension:

   Large language models exhibit an exceptional ability to comprehend and process intricate and nuanced contexts. This capability empowers them to excel in sentiment analysis, contextual translations, and handling subtle conversational nuances. Their deep learning architecture enables them to discern subtle distinctions in meanings and intentions, proving invaluable for applications in customer service, content creation, and various AI-driven interactive platforms.

5. Scalability Across Diverse Applications:

These models demonstrate high scalability, rendering them suitable for a broad spectrum of applications, ranging from small-scale personal projects to extensive enterprise solutions. Their design facilitates seamless integration and scalability based on the specific requirements of the task at hand, be it processing large datasets or adapting to diverse languages and domains. This scalability ensures that as project demands grow or change, the large language model can easily adjust to tackle new challenges without requiring extensive redesign or replacement.

In conclusion, utilizing LLMs presents numerous advantages, establishing them as potent assets in natural language processing and artificial intelligence. Their versatility across tasks allows a single model to handle diverse challenges, from text classification to document summarization, streamlining the development process. The fine-tuning process is notably efficient with LLMs, requiring minimal data for adaptation to specialized applications accelerating integration into various industries. Moreover, LLMs exhibit continuous performance improvement with increased data and parameters, ensuring they stay at the forefront of language processing capabilities. Their advanced contextual comprehension empowers them in tasks like sentiment analysis and contextual translations, proving invaluable in customer service and content creation. Additionally, LLMs demonstrate high scalability, making them suitable for a broad spectrum of applications, from small-scale projects to extensive enterprise solutions, ensuring adaptability to changing project demands without extensive redesign or replacement.

Based on a study by Zhang et al. (2023a), Large Language Model (LLM)–based conversational agents, such as ChatGPT, are widely used in critical domains such as healthcare, finance, and personal counseling. However, these applications often require users to disclose sensitive information, such as medical records, payslips, and personal traumas, to hosting organizations and third-party developers who build applications based on these LLMs. This wide-ranging disclosure brings with it emerging privacy and security risks.

The privacy risks associated with LLM-based conversational agents can be divided into two main categories. The first category includes traditional security and privacy risks such as data leaks and potential misuse or sale of personal data. Because most popular LLM-based conversational agents (CAs) run on the cloud, users lose control over their chat logs after they leave their devices, making them vulnerable to security and privacy vulnerabilities. The second category focuses on the memorization risks of LLMs. Previous research has shown that these models can memorize details from training data and inadvertently leak this information in response to specific prompts. Since current LLM-based CAs use user data for periodic model training, there is a risk that sensitive information from a user's input could be memorized and leaked in response to prompts from others.

While traditional CAs, such as Alexa and Siri, have more limited use cases, LLM-based CAs, with their open-ended nature, offer users the ability to share a broader range of information. This potential for diverse information sharing can increase both the scale and intensity of traditional security risks and memorization risks, a feature that distinguishes them from the legacy CA paradigm.

In his comprehensive analysis, Sebastian (2023) sheds light on the cybersecurity challenges of deploying conversational agents like ChatGPT. The identified risks encompass the potential reduction of entry barriers for cybercriminals, compliance gaps in AI regulations, dissemination of false information, and concerns about algorithmic fairness. Mitigating these risks involves implementing inbuilt controls, establishing regulatory frameworks, monitoring information accuracy, and ensuring fairness in AI responses.

Sebastian underscores the dynamic nature of the technological landscape, emphasizing the need for continuous reviews and adaptations of controls to address evolving cyber threats. He advocates for a multifaceted approach, combining regulatory measures, security protocols, and ethical considerations to harness the capabilities of AI chatbots responsibly. The study highlights the significance of ongoing assessments and proactive measures in ensuring the secure and ethical utilization of ChatGPT and similar AI-driven technologies in an ever-changing digital environment.

3.3 SELECTING THE RIGHT LARGE LANGUAGE MODEL

When selecting the suitable LLM for a specific application, it is essential to understand that there is no "perfect" model. Each model comes with its own set of trade-offs, and the decision should be based on a balance of various criteria. The critical decision criteria include (Databricks, 2023):

This image has been generated with DALL-E using appropriate prompts

1. Model Quality:

When selecting a LLM, assessing its quality is paramount, encompassing its proficiency in understanding language, contextual reasoning, accuracy, and coherence of outputs. High-quality LLMs are adept at comprehending nuanced language, maintaining context over discussions, generating relevant and appropriate responses, and handling complex tasks with sophistication. However, these advanced capabilities often come with increased demands for computational resources. Thus, choosing the right LLM involves balancing its performance attributes with the practical considerations of resource requirements and application-specific needs for precision and reliability.

2. Serving Cost:

The serving cost of a LLM is a crucial factor involving an in-depth analysis of expenses and resources for deployment and maintenance. It encompasses direct costs like computational power, which is particularly significant for sophisticated models requiring high processing capabilities. Infrastructure costs, including data storage, network bandwidth, and necessary hardware, also contribute to substantial financial investments. Additional expenses such as software licenses, potential upgrades, and specialized personnel for management and maintenance further impact serving costs. Striking a balance between cost-effectiveness and desired capabilities involves strategically weighing the advantages of advanced features against financial implications. The goal is to find a middle ground, ensuring the LLM's capabilities align with budget constraints, allowing practical benefits to be leveraged without compromising essential functionalities for long-term sustainability.

3. Serving Latency:

Serving latency, measuring the time it takes for a LLM to process input and generate a response, is a critical parameter in deployment, especially in applications where response speed is paramount. Real-time communication platforms, interactive chatbots, and decision-support systems require low latency for seamless user experiences, as delays can significantly impact functionality and satisfaction even in a few seconds. However, in scenarios like batch data processing or content generation, where thoughtful responses are valued over immediate feedback, users may tolerate higher latency. Optimizing serving latency involves meticulously analyzing use case requirements and balancing response speed with factors like model complexity and accuracy. This may include technical considerations such as refining model architecture, using efficient hardware, or implementing strategies like edge computing for faster processing. Optimizing serving latency ensures the LLM meets the desired balance of speed and performance aligned with its intended application.

4. Customizability:

Customizability is pivotal in selecting a LLM, and determining its adaptability for specific tasks, industries, or applications. Models with high customizability offer extensive fine-tuning possibilities, enabling adjustments for specialized domains and improved performance in tasks like sentiment analysis or language translation. This adaptability results in more accurate and context-specific outputs, ideal for niche applications. Conversely, models with limited customization are more suitable for general use but may need more effectiveness in tasks requiring a deep understanding of specialized concepts. The choice between highly customizable and general-purpose models depends on the specificity of the application. Specialized tasks benefit from extensive customization, while general applications may suffice with less customizable models. Additionally, the customization process varies in complexity, involving tasks such as training with additional datasets and adjusting parameters, requiring substantial resources. In conclusion, the level of customization needed for an LLM should align with the application's requirements, ensuring the model meets immediate needs and has the potential to evolve with changing demands.

In conclusion, when selecting the suitable LLM for a specific application, it is essential to recognize that no model is perfect, and each involves its own set of trade-offs. The decision-making process should balance various critical criteria: model quality, serving cost, serving latency, and customIzability. Model quality is critical, focusing on language understanding, contextual reasoning, and the coherence of outputs, with the understanding that higher quality often demands more resources. Serving cost requires an evaluation of the financial and infrastructural investments needed for deployment and maintenance. Serving latency, which is the response time of the model, is crucial in applications needing quick interactions, necessitating a balance between speed and model complexity. Customizability is how well the model can be tailored to specific tasks and industries, choosing between highly customizable models for specialized tasks and less customizable ones for general purposes. Ultimately, choosing an LLM should involve carefully considering these factors, ensuring the model aligns well with the specific needs and limitations of the intended application.

3.4 THE INNER WORKINGS OF LLMs: UNVEILING THE MECHANISM

Processing LLMs involves a critical phase known as data preprocessing, significantly enhancing the model's performance. This multifaceted stage encompasses meticulous operations applied to the raw corpus, including quality filtering, deduplication, privacy reduction, and tokenization. Quality filtering ensures the data is refined, eliminating noise and irrelevant information. Deduplication focuses on removing duplicate instances to enhance the dataset's coherence and efficiency. Privacy reduction techniques are implemented to safeguard sensitive information within the corpus. *Tokenization* is a fundamental step that involves breaking down the text into smaller units, such as words or subwords, facilitating the model's understanding of language nuances.

Once the raw corpus undergoes these preprocessing steps, it becomes poised for pre-training, a pivotal phase where the model acquires knowledge from the vast dataset. The readiness of the data after these comprehensive processes is visually depicted in Figure 31. This figure serves as a visual representation of the intricate pipeline of steps involved in preparing LLMs for subsequent tasks. Each step in the pipeline plays a crucial role in shaping the model's understanding of language, contributing to its ability to generate coherent and contextually relevant responses across various applications.

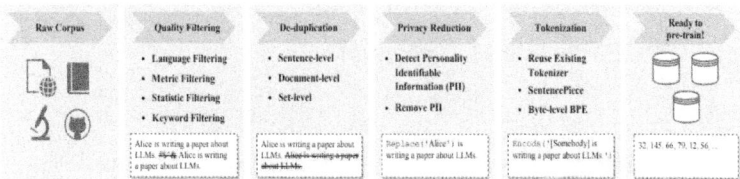

Figure 31: An illustration of a typical data preprocessing pipeline for pre-training LLMs
Source: Zhao, W. X., Zhou, K., Li, J., Tang, T., Wang, X., Hou, Y., ... & Wen, J. R. (2023a)

LifeArchitect.ai leverages diverse data sources to curate the content within GPT-3, predominantly drawing from Common Crawl, Wikipedia, books, and web text (Figure 32). The term "**Common Crawl**" refers to a freely accessible web archive dataset that encompasses a vast collection of web pages and content crawled from the internet. This dataset is a foundational resource for training large language models like GPT-3. Wikipedia, a widely recognized online encyclopedia, contributes to the knowledge base incorporated into GPT-3, providing factual information and a broad understanding of various topics. Books, which constitute another significant source, offer a literary perspective and diverse narratives, further enriching the model's comprehension. Webtext, likely comprising text from various websites and online sources, contributes to the model's familiarity with contemporary language usage and internet-based content. The amalgamation of these diverse datasets ensures that GPT-3 possesses a comprehensive understanding of language and information, making it a versatile tool for various natural language processing tasks.

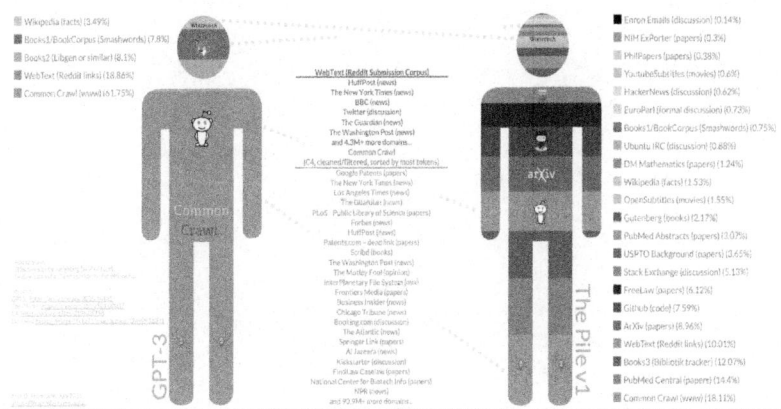

Figure 32: Contents of GPT-3 & THE PILE V1
Source: LifeArchitect (2023)

In the work by Zhao et al (2023a)., they have ingeniously visualized the composition of significant language models, including GPT-3, through an alternative graphical representation denoted as Figure 33. This visualization offers a nuanced and detailed portrayal of the intricate nature of these language models. By scrutinizing Graph Y, one can gain insights into the various components and data sources that contribute to the richness of these models. Notably, the visual representation provides a layered view, showcasing the influence and weightage of datasets such as Common Crawl, Wikipedia, books, and web text. Each layer of the graph symbolizes these data sources' distinctive characteristics and contributions, elucidating how they collectively shape the extensive knowledge and linguistic capabilities encapsulated within GPT-3. The graphical representation is an invaluable tool for comprehending the multifaceted amalgamation of diverse datasets that underpin the proficiency of prominent language models in natural language processing tasks.

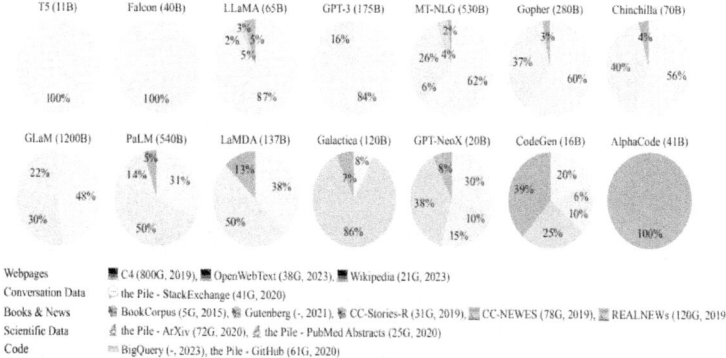

Figure 33: Contents of LLMs
Source: Zhao, W. X., Zhou, K., Li, J., Tang, T., Wang, X., Hou, Y., ... & Wen, J. R. (2023a)

Within the compilation of GPT-3's top 10 datasets presented by LifeArchitect.ai, the foremost position is occupied by a trio of influential sources: Libgen, Smashwords, and Wikipedia (Figure 34). These datasets play a pivotal role in shaping the extensive knowledge base and language proficiency of GPT-3.

Libgen, a prominent contributor, is a valuable resource for accessing vast academic content, including scholarly articles, books, and publications. The inclusion of Libgen in GPT-3's dataset ensures a wealth of diverse information, enriching the model's ability to comprehend and generate content across a spectrum of academic domains.

Smashwords, another key dataset, offers a unique contribution by providing access to various e-books. This dataset enhances GPT-3's understanding of literary content, enabling the model to engage in more nuanced and contextually relevant discussions related to literature and fiction.

Wikipedia, occupying a central position, is renowned for its comprehensive and openly accessible encyclopedic content. Incorporating Wikipedia into GPT-3's datasets infuses the model with a broad understanding of general knowledge, current events, historical facts, and various topics, facilitating versatile and informed interactions.

These datasets collectively contribute to GPT-3's capabilities, ensuring a well-rounded and expansive reservoir of information that empowers the model to generate contextually relevant and accurate responses across various domains and subject matters.

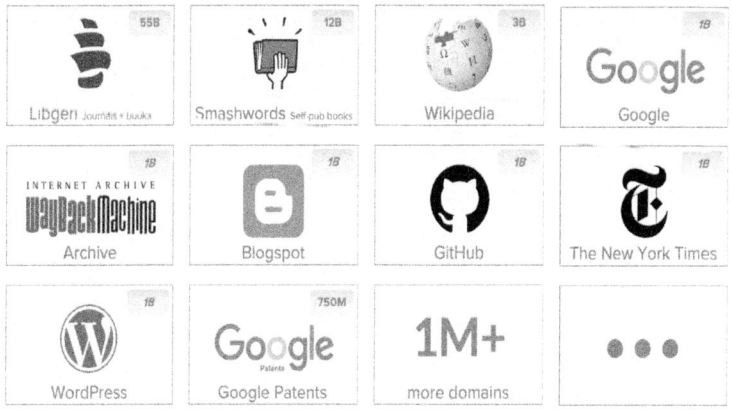

Figure 34: GPT-3's Top 10 Datasets (By Domain/Source)
Source: LifeArchitect (2023)

ChatGPT, developed by OpenAI, is a remarkable tool for generating human-like text. Its underlying mechanism is both simple and fascinating. The core function of ChatGPT is to find the most reasonable continuation for a given piece of text based on vast data from the web and other sources.

ChatGPT works by attempting to provide a logical continuation to a text string at each step. This process is described in detail in Wolfram's 2023 paper. ChatGPT tries to determine which word usually follows a given phrase by scanning billions of pages of human-written text.

Imagine you give it a phrase like "**The best thing about AI is its ability to**." ChatGPT scans billions of similar phrases and determines the most likely word to follow (Figure 35). This is done not by literal matching but by finding matches in meaning. This process results in a list of possible following words, each with a probability attached.

	learn	4.5%
	predict	3.5%
The best thing about AI is its ability to	make	3.2%
	understand	3.1%
	do	2.9%

Figure 35: ChatGPT's Text Continuation
Source: Wolfram, S. (2023)

ChatGPT generates text one word at a time to create a reasonable continuation of its given text. Imagine it scanning billions of pages of human-written text to see what word typically follows a given phrase. It does not look at literal text but seeks similar meanings. When ChatGPT writes, it repeatedly asks, "**What should the next word be?**" based on the existing text and adds a word each time (Figure 36).

The intriguing part comes in the selection of the next word. It should always pick the word with the highest probability, but this leads to dull, uncreative text. By introducing randomness and occasionally choosing lower-ranked words, ChatGPT produces more exciting and varied text. This randomness means that using the same prompt can yield different results each time. The degree of randomness, or "**temperature**," is adjustable, with a setting of 0.8 often yielding the best essay results.

The concept of "temperature" is derived from statistical physics, but there is no physical connection—it is just what has been found to work well in practice.

For demonstration purposes, Wolfram (2023) often uses the simpler GPT-2 model, which can run on a standard desktop computer. This model also uses the exact mechanism of adding one word at a time, with the possibility of choosing words based on different temperatures.

The underlying mechanism of ChatGPT is a neural network model, which can be used as a black box to predict the next word in a sequence. By applying this model to text and experimenting with different "temperatures," one can see how ChatGPT generates varied and contextually appropriate text. The process involves balancing between choosing the most probable words and introducing randomness for diversity and creativity. ChatGPT's effectiveness in generating meaningful text lies in its ability to mimic human language patterns based on the statistical analysis of large amounts of text and its clever use of randomness to add creativity and variety to its output.

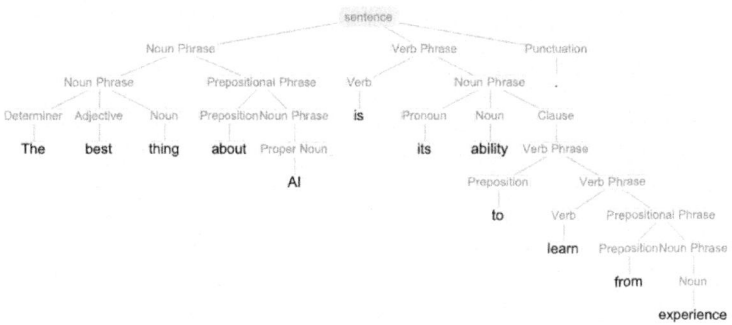

Figure 36: The Neural Mechanism of ChatGPT's Text Generation
Source: Wolfram, S. (2023)

Wolfram (2023) discusses the intricacies of human language and thought, traditionally attributed to the complexity of the human brain with its vast neural networks. The paper examines how ChatGPT, an artificial neural network with a scale comparable to the human brain, effectively mimics language generation, challenging the notion that language and thought are exceptionally complex. This effectiveness suggests that language may be governed by more straightforward, undiscovered 'laws of language' and 'laws of thought.' ChatGPT's ability to implicitly learn syntax and grammar and to make judgments about sentence meaningfulness points towards these underlying principles. The paper speculates that making these implicit laws explicit could lead to advancements in language processing, leveraging the neural network's capacity to discern language structures and regularities.

Andrej Karpathy's 2023 YouTube video "**Intro to Large Language Models**" is an essential resource for an insightful overview of large language models. It offers an explicit, in-depth exploration of the training process for GPT-like models, essential for anyone interested in the intricacies of artificial intelligence. Now, let us discuss these stages in detail.

In order to gain a deeper understanding of the training process employed for ChatGPT, we have taken the initiative to create a schematic representation of the model. This endeavor has been influenced and guided by the insights shared in Andrej Karpathy's illuminating 2023 YouTube video, ' Intro to Large Language Models.' By visualizing the model this way, we aim to provide a more insightful and comprehensive view of the intricate training procedures employed (Figure 37).

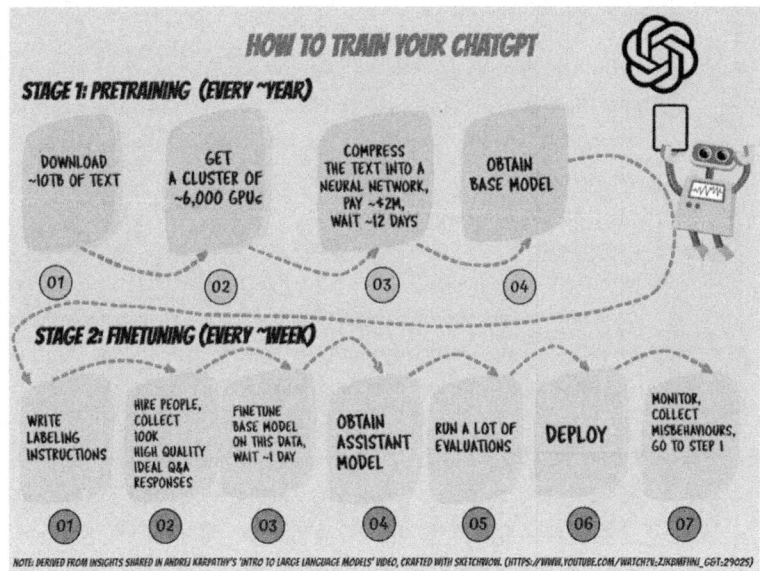

Figure 37: How to Train Your ChatGPT
"This content is inspired by Andrej Karpathy's 2023 YouTube video
'Intro to Large Language Models.'"

The video (2023) "**Intro to Large Language Models**" by **Andrej Karpathy** on YouTube is a valuable resource, offering in-depth insights into the intricate process of training large language models. This exploration lays the foundation for a more comprehensive understanding of the steps involved in training a GPT-like model, providing clarity on each aspect for individuals seeking to delve deeper into this sophisticated realm of artificial intelligence. Now, let us discuss these stages in detail.

Pre-Training Stage:

- **Data Collection:** Accumulate an extensive corpus of text from diverse internet sources. This vast collection encompasses a wide range of topics, styles, and formats to ensure the model learns a broad spectrum of language patterns.

- **Computational Infrastructure:** Set up a robust computational infrastructure, primarily a cluster of high-end GPUs. These are not standard consumer-grade hardware but specialized equipment designed for heavy parallel processing tasks, essential for handling the immense computational demands of training a large language model.

- **Model Training Process:** Feed the collected text data into the neural network. This involves training the model to understand and generate language by adjusting its internal parameters, which requires substantial computational resources and expertise.

- **Resource Intensity:** The cost and complexity of this stage are high, often involving millions of dollars. Well-funded organizations typically undertake it due to the need for significant computational power and technical know-how.

- **Outcome:** The result is a broad and general-purpose base model that has yet to be specialized but has learned many language patterns and structures.

Initial Fine-Tuning Stage:

- **Defining Objectives:** Establish specific objectives and guidelines for the model's behavior. This involves creating detailed labeling instructions that dictate how the model should respond in various scenarios, mainly focusing on the desired application, like a chatbot.

- **Data Annotation and Expansion:** Collaborate with specialized teams or companies to annotate and expand the data according to these instructions. This step often involves generating thousands of high-quality, context-specific Q&A pairs that exemplify the desired model behavior.

- **Model Refinement:** The base model is then fine-tuned with this new, annotated dataset. This process adapts the model's parameters to better align with the specific conversational goals and scenarios outlined in the labeling instructions.
- **Cost and Time Efficiency:** This stage is less costly and time-consuming than pre-training. It might take a relatively short time (e.g., a single day) compared to the months required for pre-training.

Iterative Fine-Tuning Stage (Optional):

- **Deployment and Monitoring:** Deploy the fine-tuned model in a real-world setting and continuously monitor its performance. This involves collecting and analyzing instances where the model does not perform as expected.

- **Error Correction and Data Enrichment:** Have a human expert provide the correct response for each error or misbehavior. These corrected responses are then added to the training dataset, enriching it with real-world, practical examples of desired outputs.

- **Ongoing Model Improvement:** Regularly update and retrain the model with this enriched dataset. This iterative process allows continuous refinement and adaptation, addressing specific weaknesses and improving overall performance.

- **Flexibility in Iteration Frequency:** This stage can be repeated frequently (daily or weekly) due to its lower cost and computational requirements, allowing for rapid and responsive model improvement.

Additional Considerations:

- **Base Model vs. Assistant Model:** The base model is a foundation and requires fine-tuning to become a practical tool for specific tasks. In contrast, an assistant model is already tuned for a particular function, like answering questions or assisting users.
- **Leveraging Existing Resources:** Some organizations, like Meta, release base and assistant models. The base models provide a starting point for customized fine-tuning, while assistant models are ready for immediate application in specific tasks.

Through these stages, a GPT-like model is not just trained but also meticulously refined and tailored to perform specific functions with high accuracy and relevance, demonstrating a balance between foundational training and targeted ongoing improvement.

Thirunavukarasu et al. (2023) also detail several critical steps in fine-tuning a Large Language Model (LLM) like GPT-3.5 to develop a specialized chatbot such as ChatGPT. These steps include (Figure 38):

1. Initial Training of GPT-3: GPT-3 is initially trained through word prediction tasks using a vast dataset of text sourced from the internet. This foundational training equips the model with a broad understanding of language and context.

2. Development of GPT-3.5 through Fine-Tuning: The transition from GPT-3 to GPT-3.5 involves fine-tuning the model. Fine-tuning refers to the process of exposing the model to prompt–output pairings created by humans. This step helps the model learn to respond more appropriately to various queries, tailoring its responses to be more aligned with human-like conversational patterns.

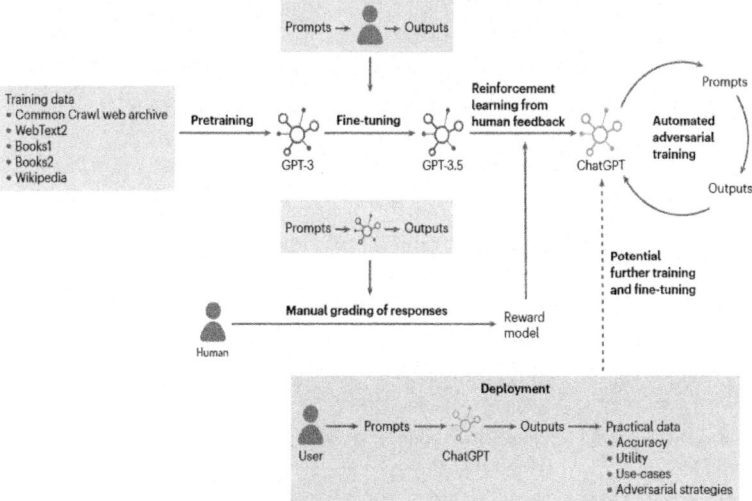

Figure 38: Critical Steps In Fine-Tuning A Large Language Model
Source: Thirunavukarasu, A. J., Ting, D. S. J., Elangovan, K., Gutierrez, L., Tan, T. F., & Ting, D. S. W. (2023)

3. Application of Reinforcement Learning from Human Feedback (RLHF): To specifically develop ChatGPT, a method known as RLHF is used. This involves a few sub-steps:

- Creation of a Reward Model: A reward model is trained using human grading of a limited number of outputs from GPT-3.5 in response to a set of prompts.

- Human Grading: Human graders assess the quality and relevance of the model's responses to these prompts.

- Training with Extended Prompts: This reward model uses a much more extensive list of prompts. The advantage here is that it facilitates training at a scale much more significant than what would be possible if human graders had to evaluate every individual output.

4. Scaling Up and Confidentiality in Advanced Models: While the specific architecture and training processes of subsequent versions like GPT-4 and further iterations of ChatGPT are kept confidential, they likely follow similar principles. This assumption is based on the fact that both models exhibit similar errors, suggesting a commonality in their underlying training methodologies.

This process illustrates how fine-tuning and specific training techniques like RLHF are crucial in evolving a general language model like GPT-3 into a more specialized and effective chatbot like ChatGPT (Thirunavukarasu et al., 2023).

In training Large Language Models (LLMs), various datasets are employed to enhance the model's capabilities. These datasets include formatting task datasets, daily chat data, and synthetic data (Zhao et al. 2023a). Let us delve into each of these categories:

Formatting Task Datasets:

- These datasets focus on tasks related to formatting, such as structuring text, organizing information, or applying specific styles.
- Examples of formatting tasks include generating well-organized paragraphs, creating lists, or ensuring proper indentation in text.
- The model learns to understand and apply formatting rules through exposure to diverse instances of formatted text.

Formatting Daily Chat Data:

- This dataset category uses conversational data that includes discussions related to formatting in everyday language.
- Users might naturally inquire or discuss formatting aspects during casual conversations, and this data helps the model grasp real-world applications of formatting in various contexts.
- Including daily chat data gives the model a nuanced understanding of how formatting is used and discussed in practical scenarios.

Formatting Synthetic Data:

- Synthetic data is artificially generated data that mimics real-world scenarios.
- In the context of formatting, synthetic data could include automatically generated examples of formatted text to expose the model to a wide range of formatting variations.

- This kind of data helps make the model more robust by exposing it to various formatting challenges that might need to be better represented in naturally occurring datasets.

By incorporating these diverse datasets, the LLM is trained to handle a broad spectrum of formatting-related tasks, ranging from structured document creation to responding to user queries about formatting issues in a conversational context. This comprehensive training approach contributes to the model's proficiency in understanding and generating formatted text across domains and applications (Figure 39).

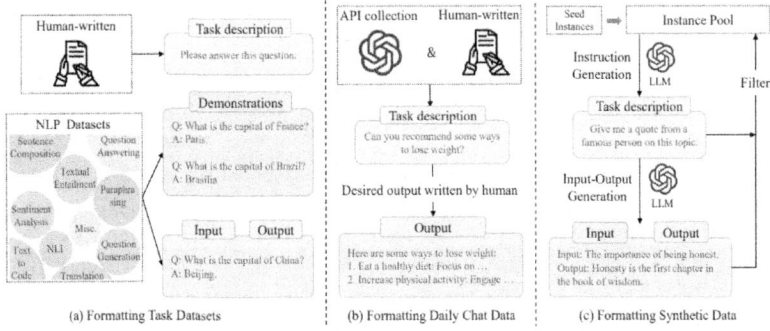

Figure 39: A Comprehensive Training Approach for Large Language Model
Source: Zhao, W. X., Zhou, K., Li, J., Tang, T., Wang, X., Hou, Y., ... & Wen, J. R. (2023a)

3.4.1   KING OF AI ARCHITECTURES: TRANSFORMERS

The journey of deep learning, inspired by the quest to mimic the human brain's exceptional system, began with attempts to emulate its intricate workings. A notable milestone in this journey was the defeat of chess grandmaster **Kasparov** in 1997, followed by another significant moment in 2016 when **Lee Sedol** was defeated in Go, a game many times more complex than chess.

This pursuit parallels efforts like the Human Brain Project, which aims to replicate the brain's approximately 100 billion neurons. In artificial intelligence, this endeavor started with the perceptron. It evolved through various stages, including Artificial Neural Networks (ANN), Recurrent Neural Networks (RNN), Long Short-Term Memory (LSTM), Gated Recurrent Units (GRU), and eventually Transformers. Each of these developments sought to imitate the interconnections of neurons in the brain and address memory challenges.

The advent of transformers marked a significant breakthrough in overcoming memory and forgetting issues, leading to the emergence of Generative AI, a remarkable achievement in the field. However, it is essential to recognize that these advancements, as impressive as they are, still strive to emulate the complexity and capabilities of the human mind. At this stage, the ultimate goal of replicating human intelligence and cognition remains an ongoing pursuit, highlighting the incredible intricacy and uniqueness of the human brain.

Generative AI's paramount strength lies in utilizing Transformers, aptly described as the "**King of AI architectures**," a term coined by Mirella Lapata, a professor of natural language processing in the School of Informatics at the University of Edinburgh. The transformative capabilities of Transformers, as symbolized by the 'T' in GPT (Generative Pre-trained Transformer), have become a cornerstone in the field, enabling generative models to excel in various applications. Their attention mechanisms and parallel processing make them particularly adept at capturing intricate patterns and dependencies in data, empowering generative AI to produce remarkable outputs. As the reigning architecture, Transformers continue to play a pivotal role in shaping the landscape of artificial intelligence, solidifying their status as the driving force behind the potency of generative models.

Before delving into the transformative era of transformers, it is crucial to trace the evolution of neural networks, including foundational models such as Artificial Neural Networks (ANN), Recurrent Neural Networks (RNN), Long Short-Term Memory (LSTM), and Gated Recurrent Unit (GRU). Each of these models has played a significant role in shaping deep learning.

"Transformers represent the future of deep learning in areas like natural language processing and computer vision."

Geoffrey Hinton
Deep Learning Pioneer

3.4.1.1 ANN

Artificial neural networks (ANNs), developed as mathematical models of biological nervous systems, gained interest after McCulloch and Pitts introduced simplified neurons in 1943. One critical development was the perceptron, introduced by Frank Rosenblatt in the 1950s, which is a type of artificial neuron that makes decisions by weighing input signals. Further developed with contributions from researchers like Rosenblatt, ANNs mimic the human brain's structure with interconnected nodes, including networks with hidden layers. These nodes, or artificial neurons, process information through weighted inputs and a transfer function, simulating biological neuron responses (Figure 40). Learning in ANNs, including those with hidden layers (Figure 41), occurs by adjusting these weights according to specific algorithms (Basheer & Hajmeer, 2000; Abraham, 2005).

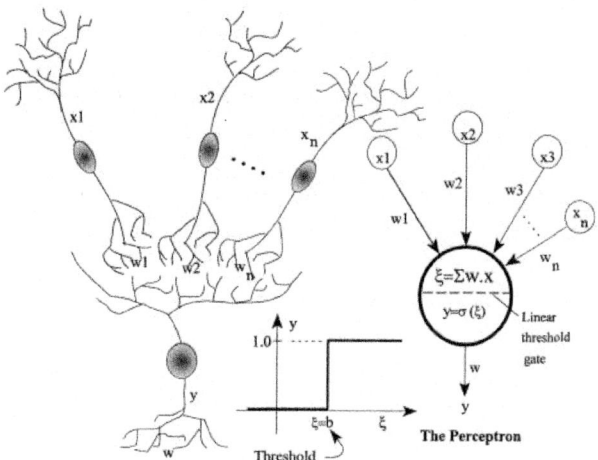

Figure 40: Evolution of Artificial Neural Networks
Source: Basheer, I. A., & Hajmeer, M. (2000)

ANNs, also known simply as neural networks, are machine learning based on how the human brain works. They consist of nodes, similar to brain neurons, organized in layers. ANNs learn from data to recognize patterns and do tasks like recognizing images or speech and processing language. Their ability to learn and improve makes them a crucial part of artificial intelligence (Zou et al., 2009; Hopfield, 1988; Yegnanarayana, 2009).

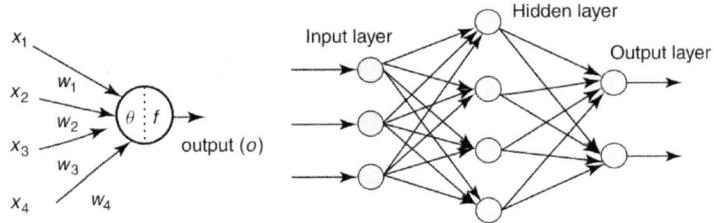

Figure 41: Artificial neuron and Multilayered Artificial Neural Network
Source: Abraham, A. (2005)

ANNs are mathematical models inspired by the study of biological systems but are only loosely based on actual biology. They function by mapping inputs to outputs, similar to mathematical functions. Designed to mirror the interconnections in biological neural networks, artificial neural networks serve to map inputs to desired outputs. However, the similarity to real neurons is as superficial as the resemblance of modern airplanes to feathers. While biological structures inspire both, the implementation in artificial systems is quite distinct from their natural counterparts (Priddy & Keller, 2005; Krenker et al., 2011).

3.4.1.2 RNN

An RNN (Recurrent Neural Network) is a neural network where neurons can send feedback signals to each other, creating a network of interconnected feedback loops (Grossberg, 2013).

During the 1990s, Recurrent Neural Networks (RNNs) emerged as a significant area of research and development. These networks, unique for their feedback or closed-loop connections, are adept at learning sequential patterns or varying over time. RNNs include models such as BAM (Bidirectional Associative Memory), Hopfield, Boltzmann machine, and recurrent backpropagation nets. Initially developed in the late 1980s by researchers like Rumelhart, Hinton, and Williams for learning character strings, these networks have since been applied to a diverse array of problems, especially those involving dynamic systems and time-sequenced events (Medsker & Jain, 2001; Salehinejad et al., 2017).

RNNs are a type of neural network designed to recognize patterns in data sequences, like time series or natural language. The core appeal of RNNs is their potential to connect past information with the current task. For example, they might use previous video frames to understand the current one. RNNs are effective when recent information is sufficient for the task, such as predicting the next word in a sentence (Olah, 2015; Sherstinsky, 2020). However, they need help with long-term dependencies - when the relevant information and its required context are far apart. While RNNs theoretically can handle these long-term dependencies, practical challenges, as highlighted by Hochreiter (1991) and Bengio et al. (1994), often prevent them from doing so effectively.

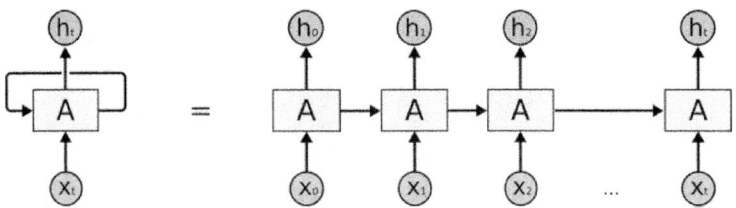

Figure 42: An Unrolled Recurrent Neural Network
Source: Olah, C. (2015)

RNNs mark a significant advancement in artificial neural networks, addressing a critical limitation observed in their predecessors. Unlike traditional feedforward neural networks (ANNs) that suffer from a lack of memory, RNNs introduce a groundbreaking architectural structure that eliminates this memory constraint. By incorporating feedback loops within their design, RNNs enable the network to retain and utilize information from previous steps, effectively overcoming the issue of memory loss (Figure 42). This unique capability makes RNNs a pioneering architectural model, allowing them to excel in tasks that involve sequential or time-dependent data, such as natural language processing, speech recognition, and various other applications requiring contextual understanding. RNNs stand out as a pivotal solution in neural networks, addressing the crucial challenge of preserving and utilizing historical information for more nuanced and context-aware predictions.

3.4.1.3 LSTM

The LSTM (Long Short-Term Memory) model, proposed by Sepp Hochreiter and Jürgen Schmidhuber in 1997, introduced a solution to the vanishing gradient problem in training deep neural networks. It became instrumental in handling long-range dependencies in sequential data.

LSTM is a pivotal recurrent neural network (RNN) architecture introduced by Sepp Hochreiter and Jürgen Schmidhuber in their influential 1997 paper. Addressing the challenges of processing long-term dependencies in traditional RNNs, LSTM is specifically designed to excel in tasks involving time series data and extended temporal relationships. Unlike conventional RNNs that struggle with information loss over time, LSTM introduces a specialized cell structure capable of controlling information flow. The LSTM cell incorporates three crucial mechanisms—Input Gate, Output Gate, and Forget Gate—to regulate the flow of information. The Input Gate determines which information is relevant to store in memory, the Output Gate selects information from the memory for output, and the Forget Gate decides which information to discard. By mitigating the vanishing gradient problem, LSTM enhances its ability to learn long-term dependencies effectively. Experimental results demonstrate the efficacy of LSTM in diverse tasks such as language modeling and time series prediction. Widely applied in natural language processing, speech recognition, and handwriting recognition, LSTM stands as a breakthrough in deep learning, offering a robust solution for capturing and utilizing intricate temporal patterns in data (Hochreiter & Schmidhuber, 1997; Gers et al., 2000; Sherstinsky, 2020).

LSTM cells, designed for processing complex time series data and long-term contexts, are a specialized artificial neural network architecture type. The core components of an LSTM cell include the forget gate, which decides what information is discarded from the cell state; the input gate, which determines how much new information is added to the cell state; the output gate, controlling what information is passed to the next layer; and the cell state itself, acting as the cell's long-term memory, carrying information through the various stages of the network (Figure 43). These features enable LSTMs to learn long-term dependencies and handle complex sequences effectively, making them widely used in fields like time series prediction, natural language processing, and speech recognition (Jenkins et al., 2018).

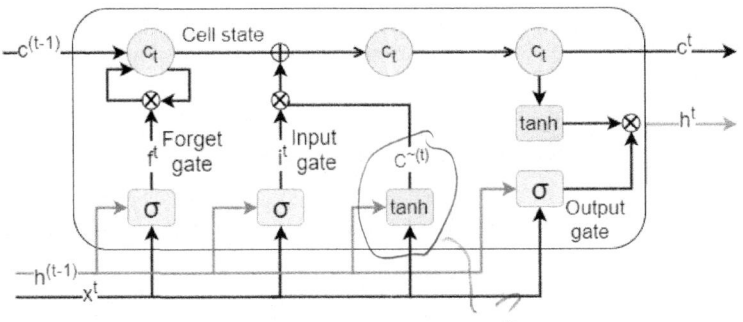

Figure 43: Long Short Term Memory (LSTM) cell
Source: Jenkins, I. R., Gee, L. O., Knauss, A., Yin, H., & Schroeder, J. (2018, November)

LSTMs maintain a chain-like architecture similar to basic RNNs, yet they differ significantly in the composition of their repeating modules. Rather than containing a singular neural network layer, LSTM modules comprise four distinct and interconnected layers (Figure 44). These layers interact in a uniquely orchestrated way, contributing to the advanced processing capabilities of LSTMs (Olah, 2015).

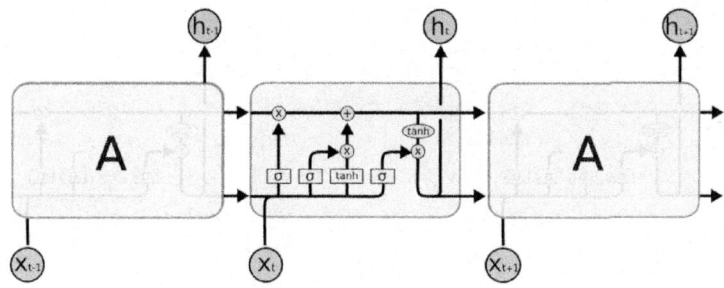

Figure 44: Recurrent Module Structure in Long Short-Term Memory (LSTM)
Source: Olah, C. (2015)

In conclusion, LSTM has emerged as a transformative solution to the vanishing gradient problem in recurrent neural networks. Its robust memory mechanisms, including the Forget Gate, Input Gate, and Output Gate, address information loss over time and enable effective learning of long-term dependencies. With a unique four-layer composition, LSTMs exhibit advanced processing capabilities, making them a cornerstone in applications such as time series prediction, natural language processing, and speech recognition. In deep learning, LSTMs stand out as a pivotal technology, excelling in tasks requiring a nuanced understanding of temporal patterns and complex sequences.

3.4.1.4 GRU

Introduced in 2014, Gated Recurrent Units (GRUs) present a variation of Recurrent Neural Networks (RNNs) similar to Long Short-Term Memory (LSTM) networks but with fewer parameters. GRUs incorporate gated units, akin to LSTMs, to regulate the flow of information within the unit. However, unlike LSTMs, GRUs lack separate memory cells. GRUs do not feature an output gate, exposing their full content (Cho et al., 2014; Chung et al., 2014).

Developed by Kyunghyun Cho et al., GRUs aimed to simplify RNN architecture while preserving effectiveness in capturing sequential patterns. Both LSTM and GRU models are proficient in handling long-term dependencies and have undergone extensive experimentation and comparison in machine translation tasks, demonstrating comparable efficiency. The choice between LSTM and GRU often depends on specific use cases and architectural preferences within recurrent neural networks (Bahdanau et al., 2014; Shewalkar et al., 2019).

Gated Recurrent Neural Networks (Gated RNNs), particularly Long Short-Term Memory (LSTM) and Gated Recurrent Unit (GRU) models have been effective in handling sequential or temporal data in fields like speech recognition and natural language processing. The key to their effectiveness lies in their gating mechanisms, which manage the integration of new input with existing memory. While LSTM RNNs utilize three gate networks, the GRU simplifies this design by reducing the number of gates to two, streamlining the network while maintaining efficient learning capabilities (Figure 45).

GRU distinguishes itself from other recurrent neural network (RNN) models through three key features:

1. **Enhanced Memory Management:** GRU provides more sophisticated memory management than traditional RNNs. Like other RNN variations, it integrates past information with the current task but accomplishes this more effectively. GRU employs a specialized mechanism to update, forget, and add information to memory, enabling it to capture long-term dependencies better.
2. **Reduced Parameter Usage:** GRU has fewer parameters than other RNN variations like Long Short-Term Memory (LSTM). This characteristic facilitates faster training and may require less data. The reduction in parameters also lowers the risk of overfitting.
3. **Simpler Architecture:** GRU's architecture is more straightforward compared to LSTM. This simplicity facilitates quicker model design and configuration adjustments. The straightforward nature of GRU's architecture makes it a preferred choice in many applications.

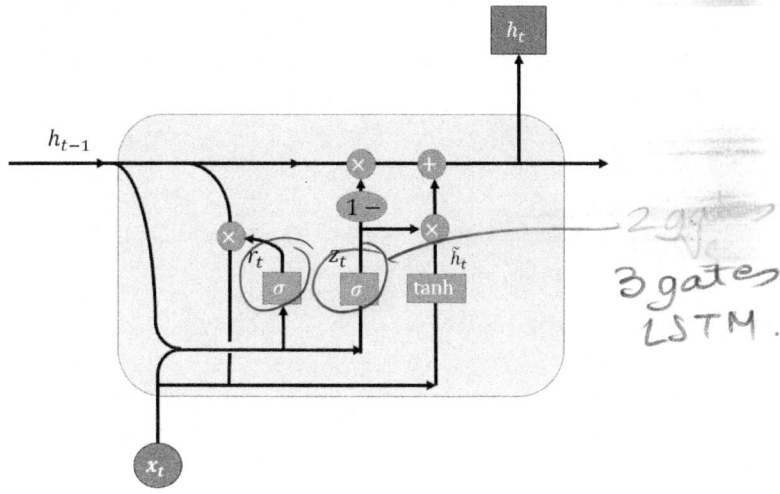

Figure 45:GRU Architecture
Source: Huang, Z., Yang, F., Xu, F., Song, X., & Tsui, K. L. (2019)

3.4.1.5 TRANSFORMERS

Transformers have emerged as a groundbreaking technology in artificial intelligence, with remarkable achievements observed across multiple domains, including but not limited to natural language processing, computer vision, and audio processing. This exceptional track record has generated substantial interest and enthusiasm among researchers in academic and industrial settings. Consequently, the research community and industry practitioners have been actively engaged in exploring, developing, and refining the capabilities of transformers, contributing to the ongoing evolution and expansion of their applications and impact on various AI fields (Lin et al., 2022; Wu et al., 2022).

The concept behind the Transformer model, which has had a profound impact on artificial intelligence, was conceived by researchers at Google in 2017. This innovative idea laid the foundation for what we now know as Transformers, representing a monumental shift in the world of deep learning. Before the emergence of Transformers, complex neural network architectures like RNNs, LSTMs, and GRUs were widely used for sequence transduction tasks, addressing the challenge of preserving contextual information over extended sequences. However, these models came with inherent limitations, notably the vanishing gradient problem, which restricted their ability to capture long-range dependencies effectively (Vaswani et al., 2017).

The Transformer model introduced a groundbreaking approach that revolutionized sequential data processing. This model comprises two essential components: the Encoder and the Decoder, each with unique characteristics.

The Encoder, the first component, is vital in input data processing. It employs self-attention mechanisms to capture dependencies across long sequences efficiently. This self-attention allows the Encoder to consider all relevant information from the input simultaneously, eliminating the need for recurrent connections or convolutions

(Figure 46). Consequently, the Transformer overcame many of the limitations of its predecessors in handling sequential data.

On the other hand, the Decoder component is responsible for generating sequential outputs, such as translations in machine translation tasks. Like the Encoder, it also utilizes self-attention mechanisms. However, the Decoder additionally employs masked self-attention to ensure that each position in the output sequence attends only to the previous positions during generation. This prevents information leakage and ensures coherent output sequences.

By exclusively relying on attention mechanisms and introducing the Encoder-Decoder architecture, the Transformer model significantly improved the performance of machine translation models and facilitated advancements in other fields, including computer vision and audio processing (Devlin et al., 2018; Brown et al., 2020). Its effectiveness in capturing dependencies across sequences makes it a powerful tool for various **Natural Language Processing** tasks.

Furthermore, the Transformer's architecture enabled parallelization, making it exceptionally efficient for training on large-scale datasets. This breakthrough has accelerated the pace of research and development in AI and has also played a pivotal role in developing models such as BERT, GPT, and their variants, which have achieved **state-of-the-art** results across various natural language understanding and generation tasks. In summary, the Transformer's introduction marked a pivotal moment in the history of deep learning, reshaping the landscape of AI and enabling transformative advancements in numerous applications.

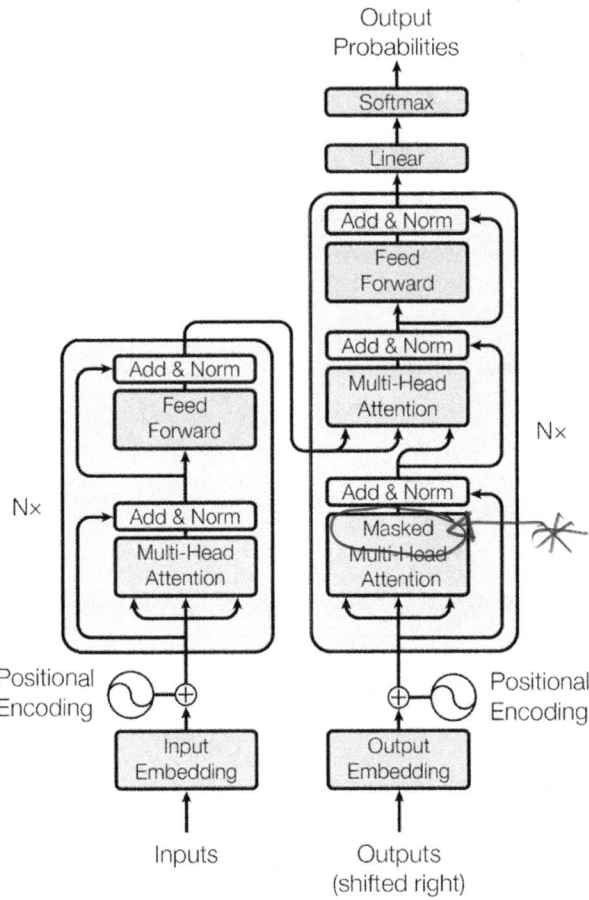

Figure 46: The Transformer - model architecture

Source: Vaswani, A., Shazeer, N., Parmar, N., Uszkoreit, J., Jones, L., Gomez, A. N., ... & Polosukhin, I. (2017)

With the growing influence of Transformer models and pre-training methods in Natural Language Processing (NLP), ensuring accessibility to these models for researchers and end-users is crucial. Transformers, an open-source library and vibrant community has been thoughtfully designed to empower users, promising to harness the potential of large-scale pre-trained models. This initiative facilitates experimentation and development on top of these models and offers the potential for breakthroughs in various NLP applications. Moreover, Transformers continues to evolve and expand, committed to providing essential infrastructure, fostering innovation, and ensuring that users have access to the latest advancements, thus promising a bright future for the field of NLP (Wolf et al., 2020).

"Generative models are a key enabler of machine creativity, allowing machines to go beyond what they've seen before and create something new."

Ian Goodfellow

Machine Learning Pioneer or Deep Learning Researcher

CHAPTER 4
ADVANCED TECHNIQUES IN LARGE LANGUAGE MODELS

4.1 RETRIEVAL-AUGMENTED LANGUAGE MODELS (RALMs)

Large Language Models (LLMs) have revolutionized natural language processing (NLP) but face limitations in handling knowledge-intensive tasks requiring access to extensive and up-to-date factual information (Borgeaud et al., 2022; Guu et al., 2020; Ram et al., 2023; Shi et al., 2023). Retrieval-Augmented Language Models (RALMs) emerge as a solution by combining the strengths of LLMs with dynamic information retrieval mechanisms. We will explore the critical aspects of RALMs, emphasizing their relevance, efficiency, and potential impact on complex reasoning scenarios.

LLMs have achieved remarkable success in natural language processing in various language tasks. However, challenges arise when addressing knowledge-intensive tasks, such as open-domain question answering, that necessitate access to vast and up-to-date factual information, particularly concerning less-known entities. Despite their considerable capacity, even the most significant language models cannot feasibly memorize such extensive datasets.

RALMs have gained prominence to address this challenge. RALMs represent a strategic fusion of traditional LLMs with dynamic information retrieval mechanisms. This integration aims to mitigate limitations associated with model size and memory constraints.

Retrieval augmentation has emerged as a promising and increasingly prominent technique within language modeling and natural language processing. Several notable approaches have contributed to its growing relevance, such as kNN-LM, DPR, RAG, REALM, MARGE, and RETRO. In retrieval-augmented language models, the fundamental process involves employing a retriever to access and retrieve documents that are contextually relevant to a given input text, such as a question. These documents are typically sourced from external memory repositories like Wikipedia or web search results. Subsequently, a generator component leverages the retrieved documents to inform and enhance the model's predictions, such as providing answers or generating text (Figure 47) (Yasungaga, 2023).

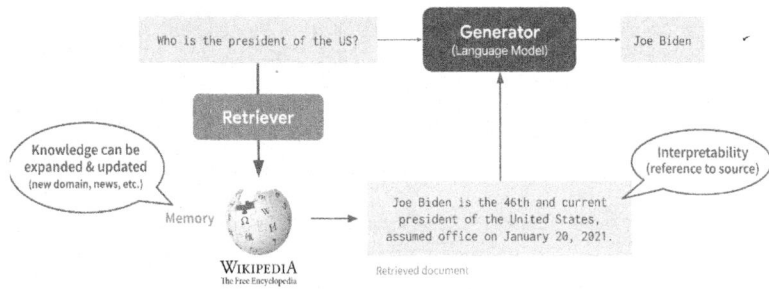

Figure 47: Retrieval Augmentation
Source: Yasungaga, M. (2023)

The adoption of retrieval augmentation offers several advantages in the field (Yasungaga, 2023):

1. **Scalability:** Retrieval augmentation allows for the reduction of model size and training costs. Furthermore, it facilitates the straightforward expansion of the model's knowledge base by incorporating additional relevant documents. This scalability aspect is particularly advantageous in managing the ever-growing volumes of available data.

2. **Accuracy:** By grounding the language model in factual knowledge retrieved from external sources, retrieval augmentation enhances model accuracy. It reduces the likelihood of the model generating incorrect or hallucinated information, resulting in more reliable predictions and text generation.

3. **Controllability:** Retrieval augmentation empowers users to update or customize the knowledge used by the model. This flexibility allows for adapting the model to evolving contexts and specific information needs, making it a valuable tool in dynamic environments.

4. **Interpretability:** The retrieved documents are a transparent reference point for the model's predictions. This enhances the interpretability of the model's outputs by providing a clear connection to the source of information used to generate its responses. This interpretability aspect is crucial in applications where model decisions require justification or verification.

Retrieval augmentation in language modeling and natural language processing has gained prominence due to its ability to harness external knowledge sources, enhancing scalability, accuracy, controllability, and interpretability in various language-related tasks. The integration of retrieval mechanisms holds promise in advancing the capabilities of language models and their utility in real-world applications.

In their study, Ram et al. (2023) demonstrate the significant impact of a simple document reading method. They also highlight that substantial improvements can be achieved by customizing how documents are chosen based on language tasks. This research shows that many advantages of RALMs can be realized using standard language models that are easily accessible via APIs. One notable approach they discuss is the In-Context RALM, which involves simply adding the selected documents to the beginning of the LM's input text (Figure 48).

Figure 48: An example of In-Context RALM
Source: Ram, O., Levine, Y., Dalmedigos, I., Muhlgay, D., Shashua, A., Leyton-Brown, K., & Shoham, Y. (2023)

One of the distinguishing features of RALMs is their capacity for real-time access to external knowledge sources and databases. When confronted with queries requiring specific, up-to-date, or rare entity-specific information, RALMs can dynamically retrieve and incorporate the most pertinent data from external sources. This capability enhances their effectiveness in handling knowledge-intensive tasks.

RALMs are an exciting development in natural language processing. They combine language models (LMs) with a retrieval module, like intelligent text processors. This retrieval module helps the LM by bringing in information from external knowledge sources. This is like having an assistant who looks up facts for you.

An essential objective of RALMs is to ensure that the retrieved information enhances model performance when contextually relevant. Simultaneously, it should not impair performance when the retrieved data is extraneous. This balance is particularly critical in multi-hop reasoning scenarios, where misusing irrelevant evidence can lead to a cascade of errors.

RALMs employ sophisticated mechanisms for assessing the relevance of retrieved information. These mechanisms often include attention mechanisms that dynamically weigh the importance of each piece of retrieved data within the query context. Such mechanisms play a pivotal role in enhancing the accuracy and effectiveness of RALMs.

RALMs are designed to prevent such information from introducing noise or confusion into the model's decision-making process to handle scenarios where retrieved data lacks direct relevance gracefully. This is accomplished through careful data filtering and contextual assessment.

Retrieval-Augmented Language Models (RALMs) present a promising avenue for addressing the challenges of incorporating extensive factual knowledge into language models. By harnessing the power of large language models and dynamically retrieving relevant information, RALMs can significantly advance language understanding systems. Their capacity for real-time knowledge access makes them particularly valuable in complex reasoning scenarios, ultimately enhancing the capabilities of natural language processing in handling knowledge-rich tasks.

How RALMs Work:

One common type of RALM follows a "**retrieve-and-read**" approach. The retrieval module bridges the language model (LM) and external knowledge sources in this paradigm. It actively seeks relevant information and provides additional context to the LM, acting as the reader (Ram et al., 2023).

The Retrieve-and-Read Process:

Imagine the retrieval module as a knowledgeable assistant that fetches relevant facts and hands them to the LM. In this case, the LM is like a skilled writer who takes these extra pieces of information and weaves them into the text it generates. This process is akin to equipping the LM with a vast encyclopedia of knowledge, allowing it to understand the context better and produce more informed and accurate text (Izacard et al., 2022; Ram et al., 2023; Shi et al., 2023).

Enhancing Understanding and Text Generation:

The retrieved knowledge acts as a guiding hand for the LM. It helps the LM comprehend a topic's nuances and produce output that reflects a deeper understanding. It gives the LM extra information to help it understand and articulate its thoughts more effectively. This synergy between retrieval and reading enhances the overall performance of RALMs across various language tasks.

So, in essence, the "**retrieve-and-read**" approach in RALMs involves the retrieval module fetching external knowledge and providing it to the LM, enabling it to produce more contextually accurate and informative text output.

Different Approaches:

There are different ways to build RALMs. Some, like REALM (Guu et al., 2020) and RETRO, start by including retrieval from the beginning. They teach the LM how to use this retrieved knowledge effectively. Others, like ATLAS, continuously train a text processor (T5 LM) and a retriever together. It is like training two teammates to work well together (Lin et al., 2023). So, RALMs are like combining a smart text processor with an information-fetching assistant, and there are different strategies for making them work efficiently.

Retrieval-Augmented Language Modeling (REALM) and Retrieval-Augmented Generation (RAG) aim to enhance language models by incorporating information from external data sources. However, they exhibit nuanced distinctions in their implementations and structures.

Broadly, REALM represents an overarching approach wherein language models utilize external data sources to enrich their understanding and generation capabilities. This strategic incorporation of external information empowers models to generate more accurate responses and reflect the latest updates. REALM establishes a general framework dictating how and when to leverage external information, encompassing diverse methodologies for integration (Guu et al., 2020).

4.2 RETRIEVAL-AUGMENTED GENERATION (RAG)

In recent times, Retrieval Augmented Generation (RAG) has gained significant traction in Natural Language Processing (NLP) alongside the ascent of Large Language Models (LLMs), contributing to enhanced performance in various NLP tasks. However, two primary challenges have surfaced. Firstly, generative models, relying on internal knowledge (weights), generate many hallucinations. Secondly, the traditional pretraining and fine-tuning approaches have become impractical due to the substantial parameter sizes and associated high update costs. As a viable solution, RAG methods emerge as promising means for LLMs to engage effectively with the external world (Zhao et al., 2023b).

RAG is an extension of retrieval-based NLP methods that combines information retrieval with language generation to enhance the capabilities of language models further. While retrieval-based methods focus on accessing external knowledge to improve model efficiency, transparency, and dynamic knowledge adaptation, RAG takes this further by seamlessly integrating retrieval mechanisms with generating contextually relevant and accurate text (Figure 49). This integration allows RAG models to retrieve information efficiently and utilize it for generating coherent and informed responses (Khattab et al., 2021).

RAG fundamentally addresses the inherent limitation in large language models: their lack of innate understanding of human language. It accomplishes this by employing a vector store, a repository that encodes information conveyed in natural language into numerical embeddings. This storage mechanism provides an expansive context and ensures the inclusion of contemporary data.

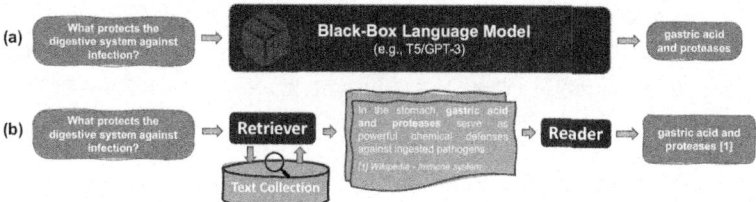

Figure 49: An illustration comparing (a) black-box language and (b) retrieval-oriented NLP models

Source: Khattab et al. (2021)

A Black Box Language Model is a language model with hidden internal workings, making its mechanisms opaque. In contrast, a Retrieval-oriented NLP Model uses information from external sources to generate text, employing a knowledge-source-based approach (Khattab et al. 2021).

RAG model is an innovative approach in natural language processing that enhances the capabilities of large language models like GPT-4 with additional, contextually relevant data. This method significantly improves the model's ability to produce accurate and detailed responses by integrating and processing extensive external documentation into smaller, manageable text segments (Jiang et al., 2023). These segments are then transformed into numerical embeddings, enabling the model to identify and retrieve the most relevant text in response to specific queries. The implementation of RAG has shown remarkable efficacy in simplifying complex technical and legal language, making it comprehensible for a broader audience. Its application spans multiple sectors, including legal, financial services, healthcare, and B2B e-commerce, demonstrating its potential to democratize the understanding of dense, specialized content. This development represents a substantial leap in generative AI, underscoring its practical utility in interpreting and elucidating intricate documents for better comprehension and utilization.

RAG is a model that combines the retrieval of relevant information from a knowledge base with language model generation. This approach enables the model to produce more accurate, verifiable outputs, as it can support its claims with external data (Lewis et al., 2020).

RAG operates by first analyzing an input and then identifying relevant items from a knowledge base that can assist in generating a desired output. This step is called retrieval, which can involve creating a search query, executing it via search engines like Google or Bing, and using the search results in the next step. The second step combines these retrieved results with the initial input to generate an appropriate response.

The model's advantages include interpretability, as it allows users to see the sources of its claims, and updateability since it can incorporate new knowledge or remove outdated or undesirable information from its knowledge base. This makes RAG more dynamic and current than traditional language models that are fixed once trained.

The significance of RAG is multifaceted. It is particularly invaluable in interpreting complex technical or legal texts, and its applicability spans various sectors. RAG delivers precise and current information across law, finance, healthcare, and B2B e-commerce domains. Through democratizing access to specialized information, RAG substantially aids users in comprehending content that may otherwise be daunting, thereby contributing to a broader understanding and accessibility of intricate subject matter.

RAG finds application across diverse NLP tasks such as machine translation, dialogue generation, abstractive summarization, and knowledge-intensive generation—notably, many approaches within this domain center on retrieving textual information. For instance, works by Guu et al. (2020), Lewis et al. (2020), Borgeaud et al. (2022), and Izacard et al. (2022) involve the joint training of a retrieval system with an encoder or sequence-to-sequence LM. These approaches yield comparable performance to larger LMs that utilize significantly more parameters.

Recent research also explores the integration of a retriever with **Chain-of-Thought** (CoT) prompting for enhanced reasoning, further augmenting the capabilities of language models (Zhao et al., 2023b).

4 PILLARS OF RAG

A RAG system comprises Large Language Models for language interpretation and response generation, Embedding Models for translating user queries into mathematical vectors, Knowledge Bases storing domain-specific information, and Indexing Algorithms to retrieve relevant data efficiently.

In a RAG system, there are four key components (Figure 50)(Sharma, 2023):

- **Large Language Models:** These models serve as the central interpreters of language and response generators. They have extensive language understanding but lack specialized knowledge.

- **Embedding Models:** These models translate user questions into mathematical vectors, enabling Large Language Models to access external specialized data.

- **Knowledge Bases:** These are vast repositories of domain-specific information, including medical literature, coding repositories, and historical data. Advanced indexing and search algorithms help efficiently navigate this wealth of data.

- **Indexing Algorithms:** Designed for speed and precision, these algorithms swiftly locate relevant information in Knowledge Bases, ensuring efficient retrieval for the Large Language Model.

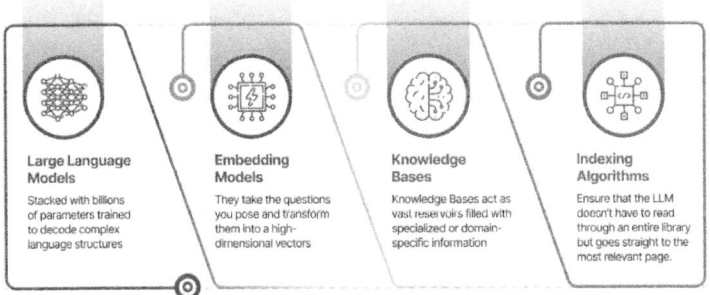

Figure 50: Four Pillars of RAG
Source: Sharma, R. (2023)

A method proposed by Lewis et al. in 2020 involves fine-tuning RAG using a pre-trained model (Figure 51) and leveraging the information available on Wikipedia. Through experimentation across various benchmarks, the efficacy of RAG becomes evident, showcasing its ability to deliver more accurate and diverse responses.

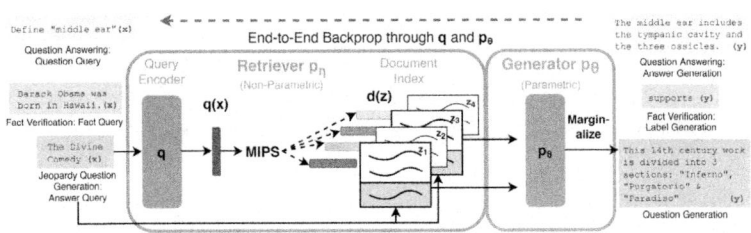

Figure 51: Fine-tuning RAG using a pre-trained model
Source: Lewis, P., Perez, E., Piktus, A., Petroni, F., Karpukhin, V., Goyal, N., ... & Kiela, D. (2020)

How Does Retrieval-Augmented Generation (RAG) Work?

The operational mechanism of RAG commences when a query is inputted. The system promptly searches for analogous vectors within the vector store, selecting the most pertinent information. This carefully curated information, combined with the model's inherent generative abilities, culminates in a customized and up-to-date response, directly addressing the user's query.

This methodology offers a pragmatic solution in terms of time and cost efficiency. By leveraging the vector store to access current data, RAG circumvents the need for incessant model retraining with the latest information.

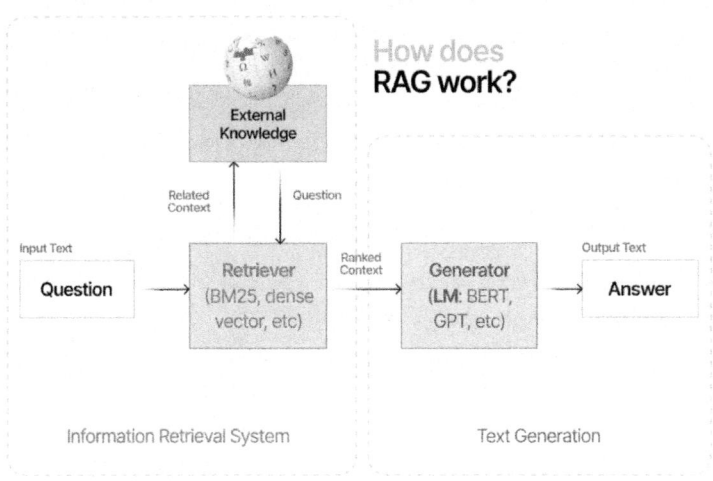

Figure 52: How Does Retrieval-Augmented Generation (RAG) Work
Source: Sharma, R. (2023)

RAG empowers large language models (LLMs) like ChatGPT to access and interact with real-time and static external datasets (Sharma, 2023). This process involves two main phases: Retrieval and Generation (Figure 52).

Phase 1: Retrieval Phase

- **Data Access:** RAG initially connects with various data repositories, including APIs, databases, and domain-specific corpora, to extract valuable insights.
- **Data Partitioning:** Due to the vast amount of data, it is divided into manageable subsets, making it easier to handle.
- **Vector Transformation:** The text within each data subset is transformed into numerical vectors that capture semantic nuances, forming the basis for machine comprehension.
- **Metadata Compilation:** Concurrently, metadata captures source details, contextual cues, and other crucial information for data verifiability.

Phase 2: Generation Phase

- **User Input:** RAG is activated by a user query or statement, laying the foundation for crafting a contextual response.
- **Semantic Interpretation:** Similar to text-to-vector transformation, the user's query undergoes semantic interpretation, generating query-specific vectors that capture its core intent and meaning.
- **Relevance Mapping:** Using these vectors, RAG searches through pre-existing data subsets to identify the most relevant ones to the user's inquiry.
- **Retrieval-Generation Fusion:** After isolating relevant data subsets, their content is merged with the user's original query.
- **Final Output Composition:** This composite data structure, comprising the user query and relevant data, is submitted to the foundational language model (e.g.,

GPT). The model then generates a contextually appropriate and informationally rich response, delivering a comprehensive answer to the user's initial query.

For instance, consider a scenario where a customer contacts your chat service to inquire about the latest cryptocurrency trends. A conventional language model, disconnected from real-time data, could not provide up-to-date information. Here, RAG comes into play. It swiftly searches through a continuously updated database of financial news articles, selects the most pertinent ones, and integrates them into the language model. Now, the model possesses the necessary information to provide a well-informed response to the user's query.

PHASES OF RETRIEVAL-AUGMENTED GENERATION

Sharma (2023) outlined four phases for implementing Retrieval-Augmented Generation (RAG): integrating a Large Language Model (LLM), refining queries for context, transforming user queries with complex processes, and deploying a comprehensive Semantic Embedding Mechanism. These phases enable organizations to harness RAG's potential, ensuring contextually informed and accurate machine-generated text (Figure 53).

Phase 1: Integration of Large Language Model

This initial phase focuses on integrating a suitable Large Language Model (LLM) into existing infrastructure. This serves as the foundational layer and often involves API integration and operational adjustments to optimize performance.

Phase 2: Contextual Query Refinement

The second phase addresses context-agnostic queries by enhancing them with contextual information. This preprocessing step transforms simple queries into more nuanced and context-aware ones.

Phase 3: Contextual Prompt Refinement

This critical phase involves complex transformations of user queries. It includes syntactic and semantic decomposition, prompt evaluation using specific metrics, contextual injection, and dynamic context-to-query mapping. The outcome is a highly contextual output from the LLM.

Phase 4: Integration of Retrieval-Augmented Generation

The final phase involves deploying a Semantic Embedding Mechanism, vectorizing the knowledge repository, indexing vectorized knowledge assets, retrieving relevant documents, and formulating composite queries for the LLM. This comprehensive approach ensures contextually rich and accurate responses from the LLM.

By following these phases, organizations can harness the full potential of RAG in LLMs, resulting in contextually informed and accurate machine-generated text.

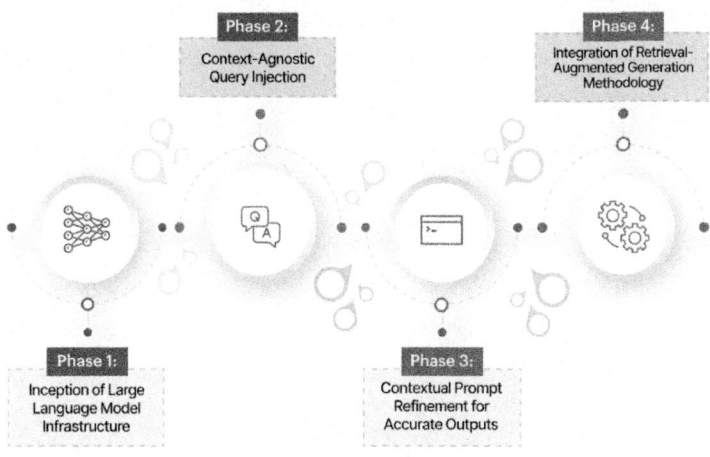

Figure 53: Four Phases of Implementing RAG
Source: Sharma, R. (2023)

RAG is a specific implementation of RALM developed by Meta AI. RAG intricately combines an information retrieval component, a retriever, with a text generation model. In practical terms, RAG takes an initial input, retrieves pertinent documents using a retriever, and then combines these retrieved documents with the original input prompt. This amalgamated information is input into the text generator to produce the final output. Meta AI's Retrieval Augmented Generation (RAG) technique proves particularly valuable for tackling complex tasks. RAG operates at the intersection of information retrieval and text generation, combining these processes for improved performance. Instead of relying solely on its pre-existing knowledge, RAG retrieves pertinent documents, often from sources like Wikipedia, and integrates them with the input prompt to generate more precise and contextually relevant responses. This approach is particularly advantageous since the knowledge of language models does not update automatically, and RAG circumvents the need for frequent retraining to incorporate the latest information.

While RAG operates as a specific manifestation of the broader RALM concept, RALM encompasses a spectrum of techniques for integrating external data into the language modeling process. With its distinctive approach utilizing a retriever and a generator in tandem, RAG exemplifies how REALM can be implemented to achieve enhanced language model performance.

RAG represents a pivotal advancement in natural language processing, markedly enhancing the competencies of extensive language models like GPT-4. This approach is characterized by its integration of contextually pertinent data and proficiency in processing voluminous language documents. Numerical embeddings are central to RAG's methodology, significantly elevating the model's precision and intricacy in generating responses to specific inquiries.

4.3 REINFORCEMENT LEARNING FROM HUMAN FEEDBACK (RLHF)

Reinforcement Learning (RL), especially with the emergence and use of large language models like ChatGPT, has significantly increased interest and popularity in recent years. These developments have sped up a significant change in Artificial Intelligence (AI) and Machine Learning (ML). Large language models, like the one shown by ChatGPT, have successfully understood the complexity of human language and made meaningful responses. However, it is essential to understand that the roots of reinforcement learning go very deep. It has a long history with many vital developments from its start to now. This history has played a significant role in shaping how reinforcement learning is today, showing its evolution through different tech periods and its growing importance in AI research and use.

This image has been generated with DALL-E using appropriate prompts

RL involves an agent's interaction with its environment to learn an optimal policy through trial and error. It applies to various fields, spanning natural and social sciences and engineering, where sequential decision-making problems are encountered (Sutton & Barto, 1999). Reinforcement learning and neural networks have a long history. Recent advancements in deep learning, driven by big data and computing power, have revived interest in reinforcement learning, particularly deep reinforcement learning (Deep RL) (Barto, 1997; Sutton & Barto, 2018).

This image has been generated with DALL-E using appropriate prompts

In recent years, deep learning, especially deep neural networks, has dominated various fields of reinforcement learning, leading to breakthroughs like deep Q-networks and AlphaGo. This trend has also given rise to innovative architectures and applications, such as differentiable neural computers, asynchronous methods, and dueling network architectures. Deep RL continues to evolve, offering creative opportunities to explore core elements, mechanisms, and applications (Wiering & Van Otterlo, 2012; Li, 2017; François-Lavet et al., 2018).

This image has been generated with DALL-E using appropriate prompts

Reinforcement learning is a powerful learning approach used in many different fields. In particular, this technique plays a vital role in developing complex systems such as autonomous (self-guided) vehicles and robots. It is also highly effective in games, and strategic games, especially Go and chess, use this technology in the background. This method represents a learning process in which agents interact with their environment and reward and punishment mechanisms operate. In this way, systems accumulate experience over time and can make better decisions and accomplish complex tasks.

Despite Andrew Ng's skepticism about the growth of Reinforcement Learning (RL) in the next three years, there are compelling reasons to contest this view. Firstly, the significant advancements in the supervised learning domain, particularly in self-supervised and unsupervised approaches like contrastive representation learning, challenge the notion that RL will not thrive. The prominence of unsupervised learning, as exemplified by methods such as CLIP, underscores its foundational role, with supervised learning being relegated to a supportive role for specific problem domains.

Moreover, RL is poised to expand and has demonstrated consistent growth. Large-scale self-supervised learning poses challenges in modeling broad distributions of behavior, requiring the identification of optimal subsets based on specific criteria, often represented by preference datasets. Reinforcement Learning from Human Feedback (RLHF) has emerged to address these challenges and has found applications in systems like ChatGPT. The bandit-style offline "RL" deployment in such systems indicates RL's growing role in handling complex behavioral distributions.

Additionally, advancements in robotics utilizing RL-based techniques, such as the recent nature drone paper, showcase RL's continued relevance and applicability in real-world scenarios. Although there is a shift toward embracing offline RL with large-scale datasets, this evolution does not necessarily diminish the potential of RL. It suggests a nuanced landscape where online and offline RL methods could coexist, with general agents emerging from extensive offline RL datasets, resembling Supervised Learning with additional reward labels.

While Professor Ng's reservations may stem from the current landscape, the ongoing evolution of RL techniques, the increasing importance of offline RL, and the continued applicability of RL in diverse domains collectively challenge the notion that RL will not witness substantial growth in the coming years.

In training Large Language Models (LLMs), the Reinforcement Learning from Human Feedback (RLHF) algorithm is employed to enhance the model's performance. Let us delve into the details of the RLHF algorithm:

RLHF is an iterative training approach that leverages human-generated feedback to refine and improve the language model. The process involves the following key steps:

Initial Pre-training:

- The LLM undergoes an initial pre-training phase using a large corpus of text data. During this phase, the model learns the underlying patterns, structures, and contextual relationships present in the data.

Interactive Fine-Tuning:

- The model is fine-tuned interactively through a process that involves human-generated feedback.
- Users provide feedback on the model's responses, highlighting correct or desired outputs and pointing out areas for improvement.
- This feedback is used to adjust the model's parameters, encouraging it to produce more accurate and contextually appropriate responses.

Reward Modeling:

- Human feedback is translated into reward signals to guide the reinforcement learning process.
- Positive feedback is associated with desired model outputs, while negative feedback is associated with areas that require improvement.
- The reward signals help the model learn from specific instances and adjust its behavior accordingly.

Policy Optimization:

- The model's policy, representing its decision-making process, is optimized based on the reward signals.
- The optimization aims to align the model's behavior with human preferences, ensuring it generates more contextually relevant and accurate responses.

Iterative Refinement:

- The RLHF process is iterative, with multiple rounds of fine-tuning and optimization.
- Each iteration incorporates new human feedback, continuously refining the model's understanding and performance over time.

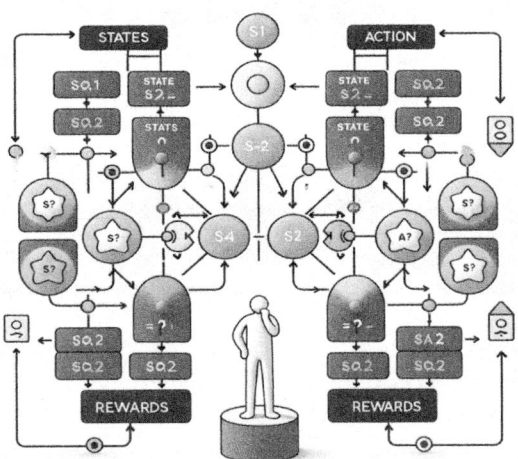

This image has been generated with DALL-E using appropriate prompts

By integrating RLHF into the training pipeline, LLMs benefit from a dynamic learning process that adapts to user preferences and requirements. This iterative approach harnesses the power of human feedback to enhance the model's language understanding and generation capabilities iteratively.

Reinforcement Learning with Human Feedback (RLHF) represents a significant stride in the evolution of machine learning, echoing Alan Turing's vision from as early as 1950. Turing, a pioneering figure in computing, suggested that educating machines should mirror how we teach children. This foresight finds resonance in the principles of RLHF. Unlike traditional reinforcement learning, RLHF integrates human feedback and reward signals, aligning closely with Turing's philosophy. Its importance is highlighted by its application in groundbreaking AI developments such as OpenAI's ChatGPT, DeepMind's Sparrow, and Anthropic's Claude. These advanced systems demonstrate the profound ways in which RLHF is reshaping our interaction with AI. The expanding success and broad applicability of RLHF not only pay homage to Turing's early insights but emphasize the need to evaluate its social and ethical impacts in our rapidly evolving digital landscape (Liu, 2023).

The alignment problem, a pivotal challenge in AI development, focuses on harmonizing human values with machine learning systems and guiding these systems to reflect human goals and interests. Reinforcement Learning with Human Feedback (RLHF), or Preference-based Reinforcement Learning, emerges as a leading solution. It has shown remarkable empirical success across various sectors, including game playing, robot training, stock prediction, recommender systems, clinical trials, and large language models. RLHF's ability to incorporate human feedback into the learning process enables a more nuanced and aligned AI development, ensuring that AI systems advance in capability and operate in congruence with human ethics and values. This approach marks a significant stride in addressing the alignment problem, demonstrating the potential of AI to work alongside human interests in a diverse range of applications (Zhu et al., 2023).

Reinforcement Learning from Human Feedback (RLHF) for fine tuning chatbots involves collecting a dataset with pairs of alternative responses, where human annotators express their preferences. A reward model is trained using supervised learning to predict human preferences, generating reward signals for the dataset. These signals guide the finetuning of the language model's policy through reinforcement learning, adjusting parameters to maximize the expected cumulative reward (Figure 54). Iterative data collection cycles, reward model training, and policy finetuning refine the model's performance, ensuring it generates responses more aligned with user preferences over successive iterations (Casper et al., 2023).

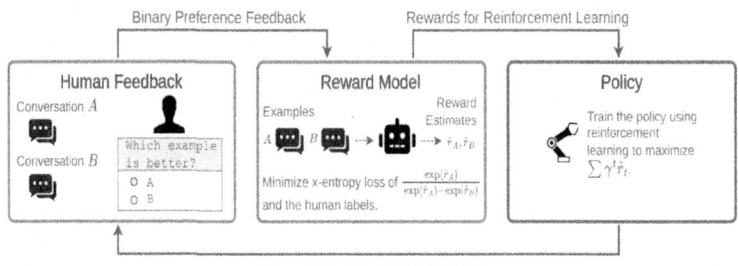

Figure 54: Reinforcement Learning from Human Feedback
Source: Casper, S., Davies, X., Shi, C., Gilbert, T. K., Scheurer, J., Rando, J., ... & Hadfield-Menell, D. (2023)

Reinforcement Learning from Human Feedback (RLHF) is a powerful method for aligning large language models (LLMs) with human preferences. Nevertheless, the significant challenge lies in acquiring high-quality human preference labels, acting as a critical obstacle that hinders the efficiency and effectiveness of the process. This bottleneck, representing a constriction in the flow of progress, underscores the difficulty in obtaining precise and reliable data points reflecting human preferences. Overcoming this bottleneck is essential for optimizing the performance and success of RLHF in refining LLMs according to human feedback (Lee et al., 2023).

The RLHF process, as illustrated in Figure 55 and referenced by Zhao et al., 2023a, can be summarized in three main steps:

a. **Supervised Fine-Tuning:**
   First, create a dataset with prompts and the desired responses. This helps the language model (LM) learn the expected answers.

b. **Reward Model Training:**
   Then, use human feedback to train a reward model. Humans rank the responses generated by the LM, and the reward model learns to understand which responses are better.

c. **Reinforcement Learning Fine-Tuning:**
   Finally, fine-tune the LM using the reward model. The LM learns to produce responses more likely to get higher rankings, improving its ability to give desired answers.

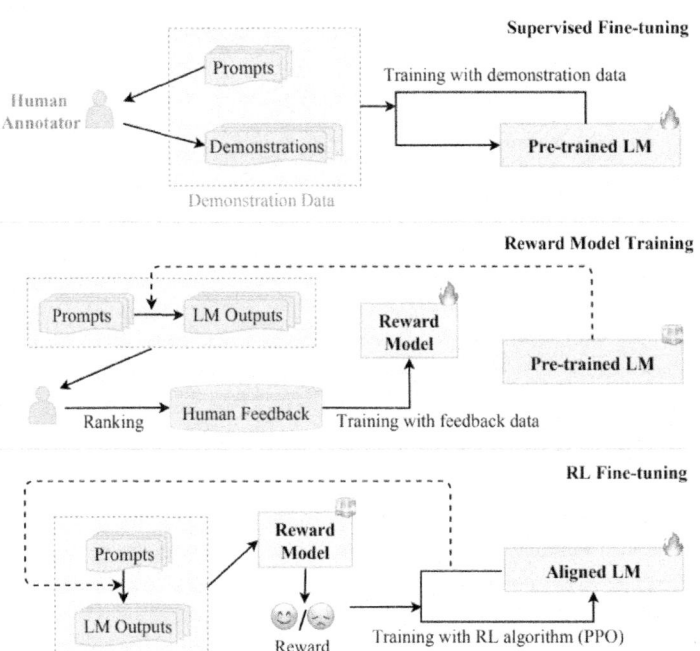

Figure 55:The workflow of the RLHF algorithm.

Source: Zhao, W. X., Zhou, K., Li, J., Tang, T., Wang, X., Hou, Y., ... & Wen, J. R. (2023a)

Ouyang et al.'s (2022) study highlights the promising potential of aligning language models with user intent through fine-tuning based on human feedback. The method involves training language models with human demonstrations of desired behavior by utilizing a dataset generated from prompts written by labelers and those submitted through a language model API. InstructGPT models, despite having fewer parameters than large language models, outperform them in human evaluations. They exhibit advantages like generating less toxic output. This approach suggests that fine-tuning with human feedback is an effective strategy for improving language models, offering a hopeful avenue for aligning them with human intent.

A diagram illustrating the three steps of Ouyang et al.'s (2022) method: (1) supervised fine-tuning (SFT), (2) reward model (RM) training, and (3) reinforcement learning via proximal policy optimization (PPO) on this reward model. Blue arrows indicate that this data is used to train one of the models. In Step 2, boxes A-D are samples from their models that get ranked by labelers. This comprehensive approach demonstrates the iterative process undertaken by Ouyang et al. to enhance language model performance and align it with user intent (Figure 56).

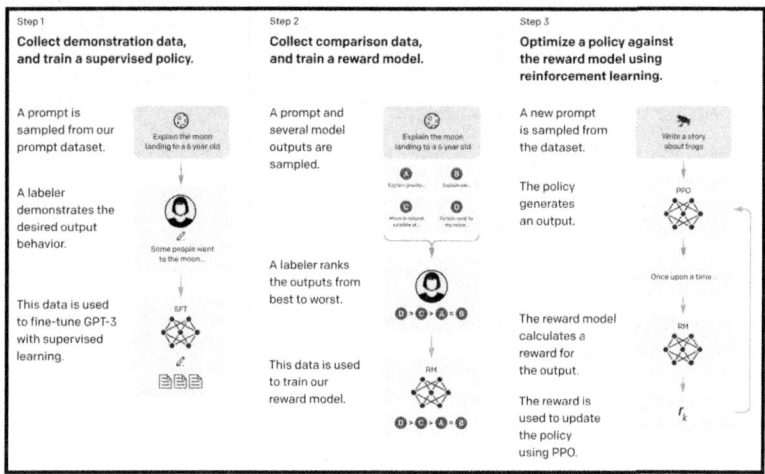

Figure 56: A diagram illustrating the three steps of Ouyang et al's method
Source: Ouyang, L., Wu, J., Jiang, X., Almeida, D., Wainwright, C., Mishkin, P., ... & Lowe, R. (2022)

4.4 PROMPT ENGINEERING: FACILITATING USER AND AI INTERACTION

As we delve into the complexities of modern software development, it becomes increasingly clear that the tools and languages we use are pivotal in shaping the future of technology. Dr. Matt Welsh discusses the evolution of computer science over more than 50 years in "Large Language Models and The End of Programming - CS50 Tech Talk", shedding light on the key challenges facing programming languages. This talk emphasizes that programming languages are needed to solve significant problems more than programming languages, especially in writing, maintaining, and understanding code. Although each new programming language introduces innovations such as more advanced abstraction and proof methods, they could be more effective in addressing these fundamental challenges. Thus, developing new languages still needs to improve in alleviating the challenges of writing understandable and maintainable code. This suggests that more than progress in the evolution of programming languages is required in terms of practical application and ease of use, as Dr Matt Welsh's presentation suggests (2023).

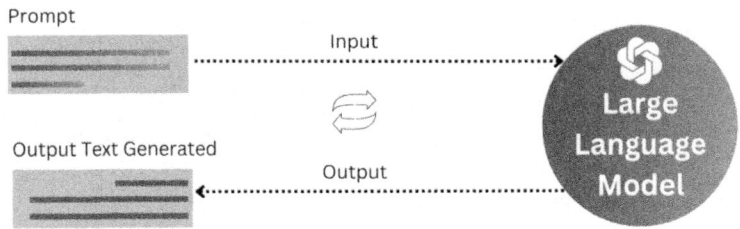

Figure 57: A diagram illustrating the Prompt Engineering
Source: Belgati, 2023. WTH is Prompt Engineering?

Rapid technological advances in computer science, especially the rise of language-based artificial intelligence models (such as CoPilot and ChatGPT), are radically changing the paradigms of communicating with traditional programming languages. This evolution drives programmers to interact with models that can make requests in natural language and quickly produce understandable code. However, given that these models have yet to reach their full potential and need more data and computational power, a critical skill set for future programmers will be the ability to use traditional programming languages and natural language-based models effectively. This offers a new perspective on how language-based models and traditional programming languages can complement each other in computer science. These developments foresee a broader communication framework in computer science and software development and point to the potential for a more effective and efficient working environment for programmers. Thus, notations and grammar rules critical for future programmers will now be expressed and developed through prompts to interact with the natural language-based model.

Prompt engineering is an emerging discipline involving the strategic development and refinement of prompts to maximize the effectiveness of large language models, especially in natural language processing tasks. This practice aims to tailor prompts to the specific requirements of language models, ensuring optimal performance in various language-related applications. As a relatively recent area of study, prompt engineering plays a crucial role in enhancing these models' interpretability, accuracy, and overall capabilities, thereby contributing to advancements in natural language understanding and generation (Giray, 2023).

A user input that elicits a response from a Natural Language Generation (NLG) system is prompt (Liu et al., 2023). Specifically, prompt engineering entails incorporating a detailed task description into our input. This approach is adopted to clarify and avoid potential misunderstandings, allowing the system to understand better and respond to the user's input rather than relying on potentially ambiguous language (Henrickson & Meroño-Peñuela, 2023).

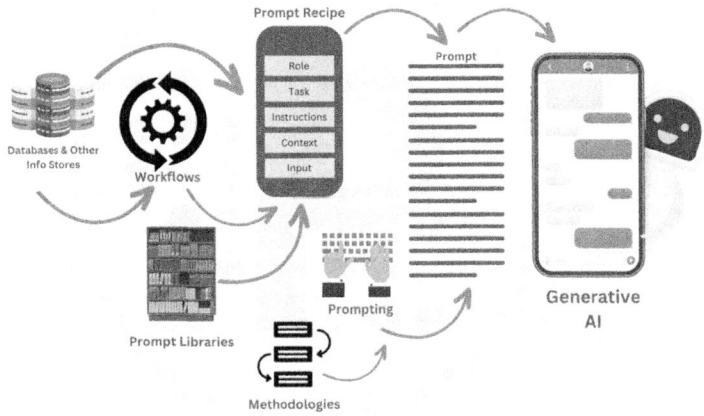

Figure 58: A diagram illustrating the Prompt Engineering
Source: Ramlochan, S. (2023). What is Prompt Engineering?

Prompt engineering is a pivotal practice in effectively utilizing language models for diverse applications. This strategic approach involves developing and optimizing prompts, which serve as the input or query to language models, ensuring they generate accurate and relevant outputs. The art of prompt engineering is crafting queries that elicit the desired information or response from the model (Figure 57- 58).

Prompt engineering is an increasingly vital skill set for effective communication with Large Language Models (LLMs) like ChatGPT. In this context, prompts serve as instructive inputs directed at LLMs, wielding influence over rule enforcement, process automation, and the desired attributes and quantities of the generated output. Prompts, as a unique form of programming, allow for customized outputs and interactions with a Language Model. This shapes the model's response to user input and improves its usefulness in different applications (White et al., 2023).

A prompt constitutes a set of instructions designed to program a LLM, enabling customization and refinement of its capabilities. A prompt plays a pivotal role in shaping the subsequent output and conversations by furnishing specific rules and guidelines for LLM interactions. This involves establishing the context for the discourse, highlighting pertinent information, and specifying the desired format and content for the generated output (Liu et al., 2023).

In the landscape of natural language processing and machine learning, the significance of prompt engineering becomes apparent across various applications. The quality of prompts plays a crucial role in determining the efficiency and effectiveness of language models across various tasks like text generation, summarization, question-answering, and classification. Well-designed prompts enhance the precision of model outputs and contribute to the seamless integration of language models into real-world applications.

Prompt engineering has emerged as a standard practice within the domain of image generation, acknowledged for its pivotal role in ensuring high-quality results (Ramesh et al., 2022; Rombach et al., 2022). The strategic utilization of well-crafted prompts has been demonstrated as an effective method to enhance the visual output in image generation processes and bolster the accuracy of reasoning within Large Language Models (LLMs). This dual impact highlights the versatility and significance of prompt engineering, showcasing its potential to improve LLMs' cognitive capabilities and overall performance. By providing explicit instructions and context through prompts, practitioners can guide LLMs toward more accurate, contextually relevant, and nuanced outcomes, contributing to the continual refinement of generative models (Kojima et al., 2022).

Prompt engineering is an iterative and dynamic process requiring a nuanced understanding of the language model's capabilities and the specific requirements of the task at hand. It involves experimenting with different prompt formulations, assessing their impact on model performance, and fine-tuning them to achieve optimal results. As language models evolve, prompt engineering remains crucial for maximizing their potential across various applications, showcasing the intersection of creativity and technical precision in natural language processing.

Prompt engineering is essential in today's AI and natural language processing (NLP) applications, making AI more effective. When you think about this concept, you can liken it to a search engine with a soul. A search engine with a soul acts like a philosopher who has read millions of books and guides you to the information you seek. This is vital to avoid getting lost in large data pools and reaching the right results. However, you can think of search engines like Google, Yandex, and Yahoo as robots that bring you the book you want in a library with millions of books.

This image has been generated with DALL-E using appropriate prompts

Prompts are like keys in this sea of information. For example, when you type "Prominent Figures in the field of Deep Learning" into a search engine, it understands the meaning and order of these words and provides you with the right results. In the same way, when interacting with language model-supported software, you should use the right prompts to express your questions and requests.

Prompt Engineering is a technique used to achieve intended results, a method that helps Artificial Intelligence applications achieve their goals. Prompt engineering is critical, especially when working with large language models. This approach creates an understanding of the language that guides how language models respond. Using an appropriate and authentic prompt enables AI to present you with the results you want more accurately.

As a result, prompt engineering is fundamental to big text data and language processing. It offers a critical approach to asking the right questions and getting results. Prompts are widely used in various applications, from data analysis to text translation, and they significantly contribute to the effective and efficient use of artificial intelligence. Therefore, prompt engineering has become integral to AI's fundamental principles and language capabilities.

The key to the ongoing success of generative models lies in skillful, prompt engineering. Effectively crafting prompts is crucial for optimizing the performance and versatility of these models across different tasks, ensuring their continued relevance and impact (Short and Short, 2023).

ChatGPT is an AI-based language model developed to create a natural language interface with humans. However, what is unique and impressive about ChatGPT is the importance of using prompts. A "prompt" is a string of text or words initially presented to ChatGPT and is used to shape the model's responses.

Prompts greatly influence what kind of responses the model will produce. A well-designed prompt can help the model understand a topic, present accurate information, or project a specific linguistic tone or emotion. Long and detailed prompts can help the model understand more content.

Prompt use improves the user experience while increasing the efficiency of ChatGPT. It enables the model to generate more desirable and targeted responses when used correctly. This offers significant advantages in the context of many applications, such as text generation, getting answers, or answering questions.

The use of prompts is an indispensable tool when interacting with ChatGPT and plays a vital role in achieving the desired results. Consciously prepared prompts help users get more satisfying and valuable answers from ChatGPT.

Prompt Engineering is strongly linked to the fundamental Data Science concept of "**Garbage in, Garbage out**." This fundamental principle emphasizes that the quality and accuracy of the input data received shape the models used in data analysis. Therefore, if the initial data is accurate and of low quality, the results can be equally complete and accurate.

Prompt Engineering plays an important role here and focuses on improving the quality of the input data. Using optimized and accurate prompts helps the model better interpret the input data and produce the expected results. Prompts clarify the user's intent, eliminate unnecessary or incorrect information, and correctly guide the model.

As a result, with Prompt Engineering, we can more effectively deal with the principle of "**Garbage In, Garbage Out**." By using quality prompts, we increase the accuracy of the initial data, contributing to data analysis and AI models producing more precise and reliable results. This is essential for those who want to increase success and achieve precise results in data science and artificial intelligence.

This image has been generated with DALL-E using appropriate prompts

CHAPTER 5
CHALLENGES AND LIMITATIONS IN GENERATIVE AI

5.1 HALLUCINATIONS

Large Language Models (LLMs), including GPT, LLaMA, and PaLM, have significantly transformed our daily lives and professional practices, showcasing remarkable capabilities in text generation (Yao et al., 2023). Despite their substantial contributions, a notable challenge surfaces in hallucination. This phenomenon within LLMs refers to the model's inclination to fabricate information or present non-existent facts, introducing inaccuracies and generating misleading content. As these models find widespread application in diverse fields, such as natural language understanding, chatbots, content generation, and translation, along with crucial industries like healthcare and finance (Rawte et al., 2023a; Rawte et al., 2023b), the issue of hallucination emerges as a critical obstacle.

Despite their advanced capabilities, large Language Models (LLMs) often need help ensuring the veracity of the information they generate. These models, including sophisticated systems like ChatGPT, can produce content contradicting existing information sources or generating assertions that cannot be substantiated through available references. This tendency to generate erroneous or 'hallucinated' information poses significant challenges in maintaining the reliability and credibility of outputs from these AI systems (Zhao et al., 2023a).

In addressing these challenges, researchers have identified and are implementing specialized methods to mitigate the frequency and impact of such inaccuracies. One notable approach is 'alignment tuning,' which involves refining the model's training process to better align its outputs with factual and consistent information. This process often entails adjusting the model's parameters and training datasets to enhance its ability to discern and replicate accurate information.

Additionally, using supplementary tools and techniques plays a crucial role in counteracting the generation of false information. These tools may include but are not limited to, external fact-checking systems, integration with reliable databases, and user feedback mechanisms. By incorporating these resources, LLMs can be better equipped to cross-reference and validate the information they generate, thereby reducing the likelihood of propagating inaccuracies.

While Large Language Models like ChatGPT have made significant strides in natural language processing, they still need to grapple with the challenge of 'hallucinating' or producing unverified content. Addressing this issue requires combining specialized techniques such as alignment tuning and adopting external tools to enhance the model's capacity for generating truthful and verified information. As these models continue to evolve, ongoing research and development in these areas are crucial for ensuring the accuracy and reliability of AI-generated content (Zhao et al., 2023a).

Hallucination manifests when LLMs produce text containing fictional, misleading, or entirely fabricated details, deviating from providing reliable and truthful information (Rawte et al., 2023b; Maynez et al., 2020). LLMs undeniably advance natural language processing, offering significant strides in text understanding and generation. However, the challenge of hallucination necessitates careful consideration to ensure the models' reliability in real-world scenarios (Huang et al., 2023). Detecting and mitigating hallucinations become imperative for the practical deployment of LLMs, as these models, despite their increasing popularity, may generate content inconsistent with reality. This inconsistency can damage user trust and pose safety concerns, mainly when deployed in the wild for applications like highly sensitive translations (Guerreiro et al., 2023).

LLMs vulnerability to producing inaccurate and deceptive information, a phenomenon known as hallucination, constitutes a critical consideration in the field. In the context of generative models, hallucinations manifest as generating words or phrases that depart from sensibility and grammatical correctness. LLMs, when assigned the task of content creation, rely on their training data to discern the intricate patterns and structures of language. However, the intricate nature of linguistic nuances and the complexities of grammar intermittently cause these models to deviate, giving rise to hallucinatory outputs (Banerjee et al., 2023; Rashkin et al., 2021).

These linguistic hallucinations can take various forms, including illogically sequenced words, phrases lacking semantic meaning, or constructions that defy conventional grammar rules. The recognition of hallucinations in generative models accentuates the necessity for a thorough understanding to refine and augment their capabilities. Researchers and developers try to mitigate hallucinatory outputs by continuously refining training data and fine-tuning model architectures. The ultimate objective is to unravel the intricacies of linguistic hallucinations, aiming to fortify the model's proficiency in generating coherent, contextually relevant content adhering to grammatical standards. This ongoing pursuit pushes the boundaries of generative language models, as evidenced by the studies conducted by Dai et al. (2022), Ji et al. (2023), and Xu et al. (2023).

Artificial intelligence systems such as Large Language Models (LLMs) can experience various challenges as a direct consequence of the data and constraints they face in their learning process. One of these challenges is the tendency to produce unrealistic or misleading information, called "hallucinations." The leading causes of this problem can be listed as follows (Figure 59) (Yao et al., 2023; Zhang et al., 2023b).:

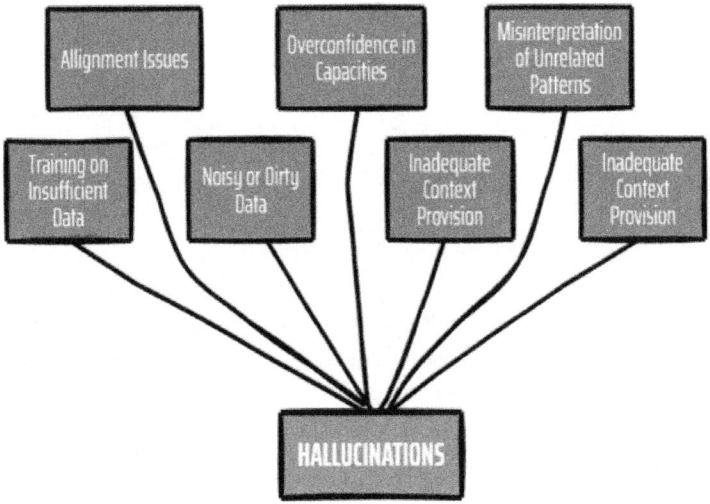

Figure 59: The leading causes of Hallucinations in LLMs

1. **Training on Insufficient Data:** Large Language Models (LLMs) are prone to hallucination due to two main factors. Firstly, during the pre-training phase, where they accumulate vast knowledge, hallucinations may arise when faced with scenarios lacking relevant information or when false data is internalized. This underscores the need for improved methodologies in pre-training to enhance information discernment. Secondly, hallucination occurs when models are trained on insufficient or biased data, impeding their ability to generate accurate responses in diverse, real-world situations. Addressing these challenges involves meticulous data curation, refining pre-training processes, and augmenting datasets for enhanced LLM adaptability and response fidelity (Zhang et al. 2023b).

2. **Noisy or Dirty Data:** The data quality used to train models holds immense importance, especially regarding hallucinations in Large Language Models (LLMs). The model learns and replicates these issues if the dataset contains errors, misleading details, or biased information. This, in turn, leads to the generation of unrealistic "hallucinations." Ensuring clean and accurate data through thorough validation processes prevents the model from producing misleading outputs during training.

3. **Inadequate Context Provision:**

   In the realm of LLMs, the provision of context plays a pivotal role in determining the quality of generated output. When the input given to the model lacks sufficient description or context, it can generate output that may draw incorrect conclusions or express unrealistic statements. This need for more context provision to be more pronounced in dealing with complex or multidimensional issues. In essence, the comprehensiveness and specificity of the input significantly influence the model's ability to produce accurate and contextually relevant responses.

4. **Inadequate Constraints:**

   The effectiveness of a model, particularly in the context of Large Language Models (LLMs), is intricately tied to the imposition of appropriate constraints. These constraints serve as guidelines for the model, delineating what information is deemed correct or acceptable. Without well-defined and stringent constraints, the model risks generating outputs that deviate from unreality or logic-defying constructs. Thus, the clarity and strictness of the imposed constraints form a crucial determinant in steering the model towards the production of realistic and logically sound outputs.

5. **Alignment Issues:**

   Hallucination arises when LLMs face challenges aligning their responses with user preferences during training. This occurs in the post-pre-training alignment phase, where the models receive further instruction-following training. If the provided instructions lack prerequisite knowledge acquired during pre-training, it leads to misalignment, encouraging LLMs to produce hallucinated responses. This misalignment may manifest as sycophancy, wherein LLMs generate responses favoring the user's perspective rather than prioritizing correctness or truthfulness. The complexity of this alignment process introduces the risk of hallucination and underscores the importance of refining alignment strategies to enhance LLM performance and accuracy (Radhakrishnan et al., 2023).

6. **Overconfidence in Capacities:**

   The phenomenon of overconfidence in LLMs, particularly prominent in larger models, manifests as an inaccurate self-assessment of their knowledge boundaries and response accuracy. Despite the ability to evaluate the correctness of their responses (self-evaluation), these models often demonstrate similar distribution entropy for correct and incorrect answers. This implies that LLMs, significantly when larger in scale, exhibit equal confidence in generating accurate and inaccurate responses. The overconfidence observed in these models is a critical factor contributing to the generation of hallucinations, as it misguides them to fabricate answers with a level of certainty that exceeds their actual understanding. This aspect highlights the need for a more precise understanding of LLMs' knowledge boundaries and confidence calibration to minimize the occurrence of hallucinations (Ren et al., 2023; Yin et al., 2023).

7. **Misinterpretation of Unrelated Patterns:**

    Hallucination in LLMs is often rooted in their tendency to misinterpret unrelated patterns as meaningful correlations. This phenomenon occurs during the model's processing of input data, where it may erroneously perceive spurious associations between elements that are, in reality, unrelated. The model's inherent complexity and capacity to identify patterns can lead it to draw connections where none exist, especially in scenarios involving positionally close or highly co-occurring associations. For instance, if the training data exhibits specific patterns or biases, the LLM may inadvertently learn and replicate these correlations, even if they lack real-world significance. Understanding and addressing this misinterpretation of unrelated patterns is crucial for mitigating hallucination in LLMs and enhancing their ability to discern genuine correlations from spurious ones during learning. Researchers and developers need to delve deeper into the intricate mechanisms behind this misinterpretation to refine model training and reduce the occurrence of hallucinations (Zhang et al., 2023b).

LLMs encounter challenges, such as hallucination, stemming from data, and constraint issues during learning. Training on insufficient data, especially during pre-training, can result in hallucinations when faced with scenarios lacking relevant information or internalizing false data. Inadequate context provision leads to incorrect conclusions in complex scenarios. Imposing explicit constraints is crucial, as vague ones may cause LLMs to produce unrealistic outputs. Alignment issues during training, where instructions lack pre-training knowledge, contribute to hallucination. Overconfidence in LLM capacities, especially in larger models, misguides them to fabricate answers. Misinterpretation of unrelated patterns occurs when LLMs erroneously perceive spurious correlations. Addressing these issues requires refining data curation, improving pre-training, specifying constraints, and enhancing alignment strategies to minimize hallucination risks.

The study, grounded in Rawte et al.'s seminal work (2023), extensively examines the intricate interplay between hallucinations in Large Language Models (LLMs) and the nuances of prompt language details. Expanding upon Rawte et al.'s insights, it reveals a correlation between higher readability and a decrease in hallucinatory episodes while also underscoring the dampening effect of formal language on such content. This investigation sheds light on the profound influence of prompt linguistics, particularly in advanced LLMs like GPT-4, echoing the findings of Rawte et al. Furthermore, the study accentuates the effectiveness of using specific and concrete terms in prompts, which proves highly effective in reducing hallucinations, especially in areas like Numbers and Acronyms. As Rawte et al.'s exploration has shown, the impact of concrete prompts grows more evident in sophisticated LLMs, paving the way for further exploration and progress in understanding and improving language generation in these models. This research contributes to scholarly discussions, providing valuable insights to improve language models and guide future research.

5.2 CONTEXT WINDOWS

Context Windows refers to the contextual information or input window a language model considers when generating predictions or responses. It represents the preceding words or tokens that the model takes into account to comprehend and respond to the given input.

In assessing Large Language Models (LLMs) capabilities using Context Windows, the language model Claude 2 has demonstrated notable proficiency. Claude 2's strong performance in Context Windows suggests its effectiveness in leveraging and interpreting contextual information (Figure 60). The model showcases a capability to generate contextually relevant responses and exhibit a nuanced understanding of the input, contributing to more coherent language generation.

The success of Claude 2 in utilizing Context Windows highlights its ability to capture and utilize contextual dependencies effectively. This proficiency allows Claude 2 to generate responses that reflect a comprehensive understanding of the given context. It is a robust model for tasks requiring nuanced language generation based on contextual information within a specific input window.

The resounding sentiment of "**the bigger, the better**" in the context of language models is also attributed to Mirella Lapata. This philosophy reflects the notable trend since 2018, witnessing a substantial increase in the sizes of language models. Technological advancements, particularly in training data, have spurred the development of larger and more intricate models, aiming to amplify their capacity for comprehending, generating, and manipulating text on an unprecedented scale. Lapata's insight underscores the industry's steadfast commitment to pushing the boundaries of language model capabilities, ushering in an era where extensive datasets redefine the possibilities of natural language processing.

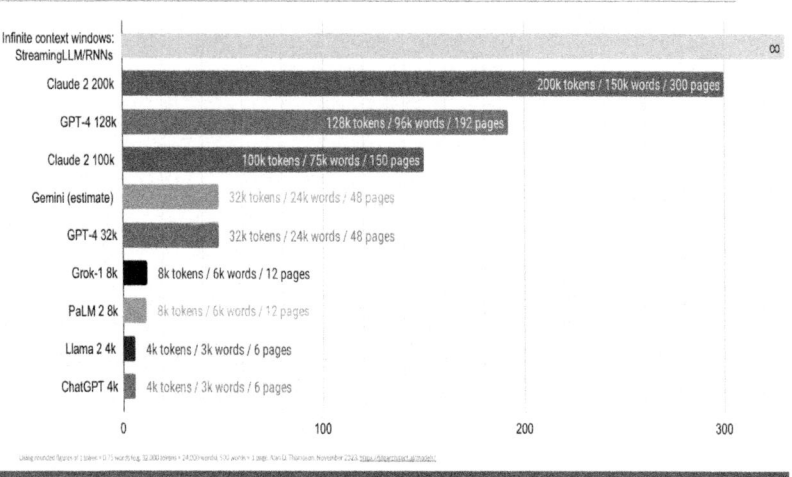

Figure 60: 2023 Context Windows (Max In/Out Lenght)
Source: LifeArchitect.ai

"Generative AI is the most powerful tool for creativity that has ever been created. It has the potential to unleash a new era of human innovation."

Elon Musk
Founder, CEO, and chief engineer of SpaceX
CEO and product architect of Tesla, Inc.
Owner and CTO of X, formerly Twitter

CHAPTER 6
GENERATIVE AI'S IMPACT ON ECONOMIC EVOLUTION

6.1 THE ROLE OF GENERATIVE AI IN ECONOMIC EVOLUTION

ChatGPT and its counterparts have captured global attention, distinguishing themselves from entities like AlphaGo due to their widespread applicability. Their versatility enables almost anyone to communicate and create content, mainly through their remarkable conversational abilities. Contemporary generative AI applications exhibit proficiency in routine tasks like data organization and classification. However, they can produce written content, compose music, and generate digital art that has garnered significant attention, prompting widespread experimentation. Consequently, a more extensive array of stakeholders is now contending with the implications of generative AI on both business and society, often navigating this landscape without adequate contextual understanding to inform their decisions (Chui et al., 2023).

Generative AI's impact on productivity can contribute trillions of dollars to the global economy. Recent research estimates a yearly addition of $2.6 trillion to $4.4 trillion across 63 analyzed use cases, representing a 15 to 40 percent increase in the overall impact of artificial intelligence. About 75 percent of this value is expected in customer operations, marketing and sales, software engineering, and R&D. This transformative technology is projected to significantly affect various industries, with banking, high tech, and life sciences standing out. Generative AI could reshape work dynamics by automating 60 to 70 percent of employees' current activities, particularly in knowledge-intensive occupations. Workforce transformation is expected to accelerate, with half of today's work activities potentially automated between 2030 and 2060. While Generative AI has the potential to enhance labor productivity by 0.1 to 0.6 percent annually through 2040, investments in worker support and skill development are crucial. The full realization of Generative AI's benefits will require addressing risks, determining necessary workforce skills, and rethinking core business processes. The technology's promising future calls for strategic leadership and proactive measures in managing its implementation (Chui et al., 2023).

Generative AI marks a notable stride in the evolution of artificial intelligence, prompting **McKinsey** to explore its potential impact on the economy and society. Through a dual lens approach, **McKinsey** (2023) assessed where generative AI could deliver significant value and the extent of this value. The first lens involves scrutinizing specific use cases for McKinsey's adoption of generative AI, defining a "**use case**" as its targeted application to a particular business challenge, yielding measurable outcomes. For instance, in marketing, generative AI could create personalized content, potentially reducing content generation costs and increasing revenue through more effective, higher-quality content. McKinsey's analysis identified 63 use cases across 16 business functions, indicating a potential economic benefit ranging from **$2.6 trillion to $4.4 trillion** annually when applied across industries.

This estimated value would contribute 15 to 40 percent to the existing economic value ($11 trillion to $17.7 trillion) generated by non-generative artificial intelligence and analytics. The second lens delves into the impact of McKinsey's generative AI on the work activities of approximately 850 occupations. Through scenario modeling, McKinsey assessed when generative AI could perform over 2,100 detailed work activities, comprising tasks across the global workforce. This analysis aims to estimate the current capabilities of McKinsey's generative AI and their potential influence on labor productivity throughout diverse occupations worldwide (Figure 61).

McKinsey's exploration underscores the transformative potential of Generative AI, signifying a substantial impact on the economy and society. This innovation is anticipated to contribute significantly to the existing impact of non-generative AI. Furthermore, McKinsey's assessment of its influence on diverse work activities across occupations highlights its crucial role in shaping global labor productivity.

Figure 61: Potential Impact of Generative AI
Source: McKinsey (2023)

Generative AI, a rapidly advancing technology, showcases immense potential; however, **McKinsey's recent report** (2023) underscores that the majority of AI's overall value still originates from other applications discussed in prior analyses. Traditional advanced-analytics and machine learning algorithms remain highly effective, particularly in numerical and optimization tasks across various industries. While generative AI is evolving, promising new frontiers in creativity and innovation, its current impact on overall AI potential is not the primary driver. McKinsey's analysis, focused on 16 business functions, reveals that customer operations, marketing and sales, software engineering, and research and development could collectively contribute approximately 75 percent of the total annual value from generative AI use cases (Figure 62).

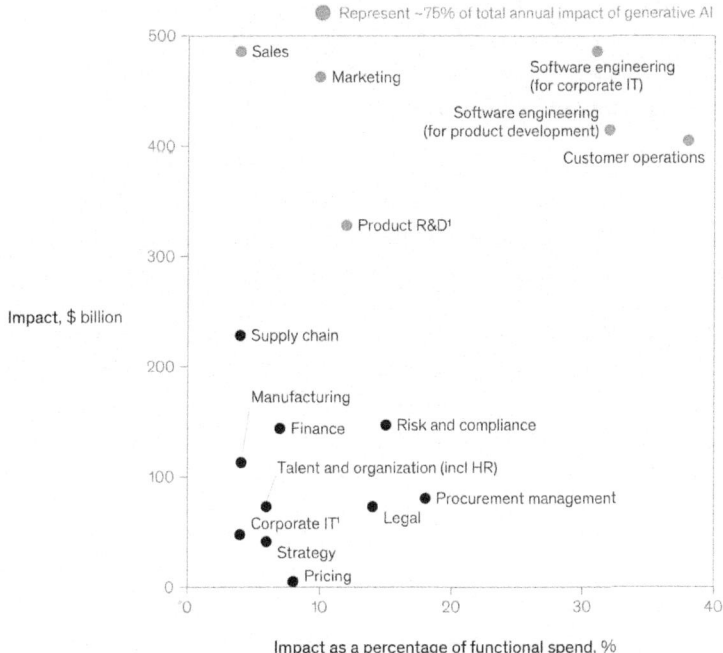

Figure 62: Potential Impact of Generative AI on business functions
Source: McKinsey (2023)

In a comprehensive analysis, drawing upon insights from McKinsey & Company's research, 63 distinct use cases of generative artificial intelligence (AI) were explored. This study highlights that generative AI possesses the potential to create an economic impact of staggering proportions, estimated between $2.6 trillion and $4.4 trillion across various industries. However, the most significant impact is anticipated in software engineering and education.

In software engineering, McKinsey's insights suggest that generative AI will revolutionize development processes. This includes automating complex coding tasks, optimizing algorithms, preemptively identifying system vulnerabilities, enhancing efficiency, and reducing operational costs.

Similarly, McKinsey's research indicates that generative AI will transform teaching methodologies and learning experiences in the education sector. This involves offering personalized learning paths, developing interactive educational content, and providing adaptive intelligent tutoring systems tailored to individual learning styles and paces.

While the overall impact of generative AI will vary based on factors such as the relevance of different functions and the revenue scale of each industry, its transformative potential is particularly pronounced in software engineering and education. This potential, as identified and underscored by McKinsey's extensive research, positions generative AI as a pivotal force in shaping the future of these sectors, heralding significant advancements in both technological development and educational practices.

McKinsey envisions generative AI revolutionizing software engineering by automating coding tasks and enhancing efficiency. In education, it transforms teaching methods with personalized learning paths. This transformative potential, highlighted by McKinsey, positions generative AI as a critical force in shaping the future of these sectors.

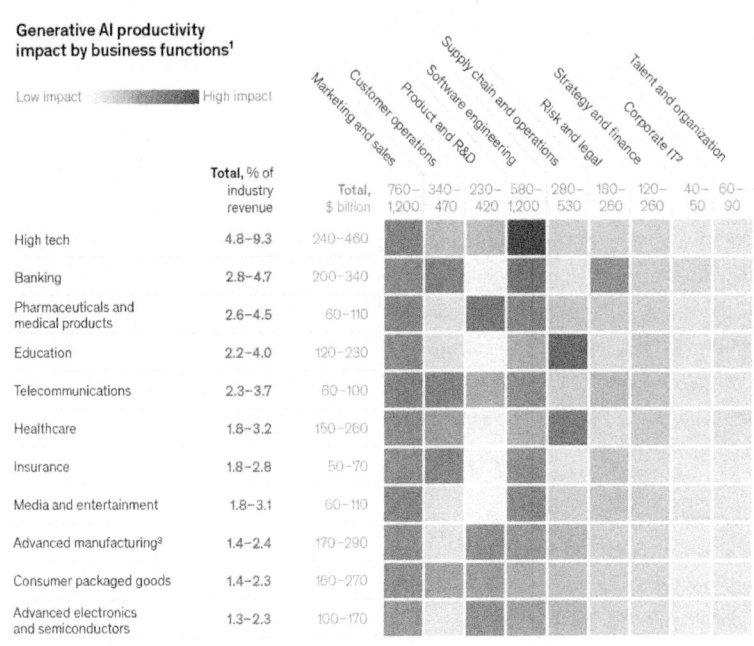

Table 1 : Generative AI use cases will have different impacts on
business functions across industries
Source: McKinsey (2023)

According to the McKinsey report of 2023, use cases of Generative AI will have varying impacts on business functions across industries. As outlined in the report, the effects of these artificial intelligence applications on business processes and industries have been thoroughly examined (Table 1).

The recent advent of generative artificial intelligence (AI) has sparked significant interest due to its potential for task automation, which could lead to considerable labor cost savings and increased productivity. Despite uncertainties surrounding its full capabilities, generative AI's proficiency in producing human-like content and enhancing human-machine interactions indicates substantial macroeconomic effects. Research indicates that nearly two-thirds of current jobs in the US and Europe could be affected by AI automation, potentially automating up to a quarter of all work tasks and impacting the equivalent of 300 million full-time jobs globally. Historically, job displacement due to automation has been counterbalanced by new job creation and the emergence of new occupations, suggesting a potential productivity boom and substantial economic growth. In the United States, generative AI is estimated to raise annual labor productivity growth by nearly 1.5 percentage points over a decade, with a global impact that could increase annual GDP by 7%, highlighting the profound economic potential of generative AI (Hatzius, 2023).

The advent of Generative AI (GAI) is ushering in a transformative era in the economy and job market, akin to the profound impact witnessed with the introduction of the Internet. The adoption of GAI technologies is poised to give rise to new professions, spanning highly specialized roles and those requiring less specialization. This transformative shift is already underway. As the level of maturity and trust in GAI technologies reaches a critical tipping point, several professions may undergo augmentation or even complete replacement by GAI applications. The future dynamics may be influenced by the prevailing business models, where humans could either become a premium tier or, in a more dystopian scenario, a more affordable yet lower-quality alternative to GAI. Specific industries, particularly in the news and publishing sector, have initiated restructuring activities, citing the technological shift and the increasing adoption of AI, leading to workforce restructuring and potential job displacement. This evolving landscape necessitates carefully examining the socio-economic implications and ethical considerations surrounding the integration of GAI into various sectors (Orchard & Tasiemski, 2023).

According to analysts at UBS, Generative AI is poised to impact the financial sector significantly, particularly in reducing operational costs. In the financial industry, where staff expenses constitute a substantial portion of total costs, the integration of generative AI technologies promises efficiency and cost-effectiveness. What sets the financial sector apart is that, unlike some other industries, generative AI is not primarily utilized for revenue generation but rather for optimizing operational expenses. UBS research underscores that the value observed thus far in the financial sector stems from the substantial reduction in costs facilitated by implementing generative AI technologies. As financial institutions increasingly explore and adopt these technologies, the emphasis on cost-cutting through enhanced automation and efficiency is expected to reshape the landscape of financial services (Table 2).

	Revenues	Costs	Competition
Banks	Neutral	Reduction	Increase
Exchange & financial business services	Increase	Reduction	Increase
Fintech & payments	Neutral	Reduction	Increase
Insurance	Reduction	Reduction	Increase
Real estate	Increase	Reduction	Neutral
Wealth & asset managers	Neutral	Reduction	Increase

Table 2 : Generative AI to Lower Financial Sector Costs
Source: MIT Technology Review Insights (2023)

The comprehensive analysis conducted by UBS analysts across 31 sectors indicates that substantial cost savings are the primary and most probable outcome of advancements in generative AI. Across various industries, the predominant impact of generative AI is identified as a means of reducing costs rather than fostering income generation. This trend is consistently observed throughout the financial sector, encompassing banking, wealth management, insurance, and payments.

The cost savings in these sectors are primarily attributed to using technology, specifically generative AI, to alleviate human employees from the arduous task of analyzing extensive and often unstructured data. Additionally, generative AI facilitates output production in response to natural language directives, contributing significantly to operational efficiency and cost reduction in diverse financial industry segments (Figure 59).

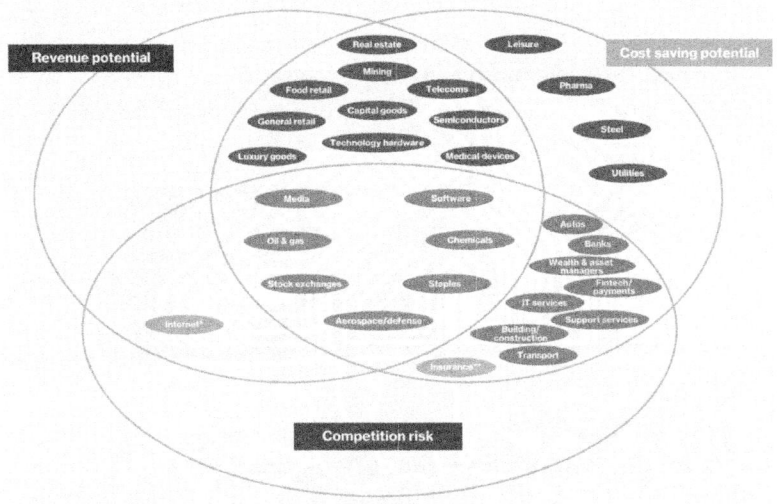

Figure 63: General Impact of generative AI
Source: MIT Technology Review Insights (2023)

6.2 COST INTUITION OF GENERATIVE AI

The "**Generative AI for Everyone**" course by Andrew Ng from DeepLearning.AI provides a detailed exploration of the cost implications of incorporating large language models (LLMs) in software applications. The course delves into specific pricing examples for various LLMs, including OpenAI/GPT3.5, GPT4, Google's PaLM 2, and Amazon's Titan Lite.

Andrew Ng introduces the concept of tokens, loosely equated to words, where common words are generally counted as one token and less frequent words might be split into sub-parts. The pricing structure is based on the number of tokens, and he emphasizes the cost of generating output tokens rather than input tokens (prompt length). OpenAI/GPT3.5, for instance, charges $0.002 per 1,000 tokens, which translates to 0.2 cents for the same amount. In contrast, GPT4 costs six cents per 1,000 tokens.

The course proceeds to demonstrate cost calculations using different token rates. Practical scenarios are considered, such as estimating the expense of keeping a team member engaged for an hour. Andrew Ng factors in adult reading speed, prompting costs, and output generation costs to estimate the overall expenditure. For instance, generating 40,000 tokens (approximately 30,000 words) at $0.002 per 1,000 tokens would cost 40 times that, resulting in eight cents (Table 3).

The course suggests that, despite initial perceptions, utilizing LLMs for various applications may be more cost-effective than commonly perceived. This is particularly relevant when considering the context of minimum wage rates in the United States. This nuanced exploration provides valuable insights into the practical, economical, and token-based aspects of leveraging Generative AI in software development.

	OpenAI/GPT3.5	OpenAI/GPT4	Google/PaLM 2	Amazon/Titan Lite
Input tokens	$0.0015/1K tokens	$0.03/1K tokens	$0.0005/1K tokens	$0.0003/1K tokens
Output tokens	$0.002/1K tokens	$0.06/1K tokens	$0.0005/1K tokens	$0.0004/1K tokens

What is a token?

the example Andrew	1 token
translate programming	2 tokens
tonkotsu	4 tokens

Roughly, 1 token = 3/4 words

Table 3: Cost-Effectiveness of Andrew Ng's Large Language Model (LLM)
Source: Deep Learning.AI. (2023)

Andrew Ng expresses optimism about the transformative potential of AI in building a more intelligent world. He defines *intelligence* as the ability to apply knowledge and skills for sound decision-making. While human intelligence is costly to develop, AI promises to make intelligence accessible to everyone at a low cost. This democratization of intelligence could revolutionize industries and address significant global challenges such as climate change and pandemics.

Andrew Ng's perspective on the transformative power of AI extends beyond its intelligence applications. His vision is that AI, particularly Large Language Models (LLMs), can be a cost-effective tool for achieving widespread intelligence. In the pursuit of building a more intelligent world, Ng highlights AI's potential to democratize intelligence access, making it affordable and accessible to a broader audience. This table aims to provide a visual representation of the cost-effectiveness of Andrew Ng's LLM, emphasizing its potential impact on various sectors and industries. By illustrating the economic viability of this approach, we encourage a broader exploration of AI's transformative possibilities and its ability to shape a brighter and more inclusive future.

This image has been generated with DALL-E using appropriate prompts

An analysis of the cost of AI replacing human labor in software development, as discussed in "**Large Language Models and The End of Programming - CS50 Tech Talk with Dr. Matt Welsh**," reveals a potentially significant shift in the industry. In areas like Silicon Valley or Seattle, a software engineer's total annual compensation, including salary and benefits, amounts to approximately $312,000. In stark contrast, the daily cost of using an AI model like GPT-3 for similar tasks is a mere $0.12. This represents a cost difference of about 10,000 times, indicating a significant transformation for software development.

This image has been generated with DALL-E using appropriate prompts

This calculation can be considered as a harbinger of a revolution in the software industry. Artificial intelligence's efficiency and cost advantages must be addressed in a field that requires high education and expertise. Unlike humans, artificial intelligence does not need to take breaks, does not have to wait for extra advantages, and can produce code constantly at every stage. In addition, although there is a risk of making mistakes, it offers the opportunity for continuous improvement and development thanks to its ability to correct errors quickly.

Another critical point this change will bring is the restructuring of software development processes. In the future, product managers and other human employees may take on the task of reviewing and approving the codes produced by artificial intelligence. However, the role and necessity of humans in this process may decrease. Regardless of humans' difficulties in managing complex code bases, AI can generate the required code, simplifying development processes.

As a result, this cost analysis and the potential brought by artificial intelligence signal a severe transformation of the software development industry towards reducing the human workforce and a more dominant role for artificial intelligence. The speed and impact of this change may necessitate the development of new strategies and approaches for professionals and educational institutions in the sector.

"Generative AI is the key to solving some of the world's biggest problems, such as climate change, poverty, and disease. It has the potential to make the world a better place for everyone."

Mark Zuckerberg
Founder, chairman and CEO of Meta

CONCLUSION

As we draw this book to a close, it is essential to acknowledge the astonishing capabilities of generative AI, which has produced almost magical results in a remarkably short time. This technology, much like a modern-day sorcerer, has the power to amaze and inspire with its creations. However, behind this facade of enchantment lies a robust foundation of mathematics and statistics.

As we navigate our daily tasks, computers tirelessly work around the clock, delving into the data we produce. They strive to grasp the intricate relationships between words and endeavor to comprehend the content of images. This relentless pursuit by machines to understand and interpret our world signifies a monumental shift in how we interact with technology. Generative AI stands at the forefront of this transformation, continuously learning and evolving, bridging the gap between human creativity and machine intelligence.

This duality of generative AI – its ability to dazzle on the surface while deeply rooted in analytical rigor – is a testament to the extraordinary advancements in the field. It underscores the importance of understanding the intricate mechanisms that drive these technologies. As we marvel at the products of generative AI, we remain keenly aware of the complex mathematical and statistical principles that form its backbone. This balance of wonder and knowledge is crucial as we navigate the future of AI, appreciating its magic while respecting the science that makes it possible.

In the concluding thoughts of this book, it is essential to reflect upon the profound insights shared by Andrew Ng, a notable figure in the field of artificial intelligence. Ng draws a compelling parallel between AI and electricity, highlighting AI as the new electricity with immense potential to revolutionize every industry and aspect of human life. Just as electricity, in its nascent stages, sparked fears of electrocution and fires, AI today is met with similar apprehensions regarding its flaws and potential to cause harm.

However, Ng astutely observes that the fears associated with electricity have significantly diminished over time, and it has become an indispensable part of our daily lives. Similarly, he argues that while AI currently has its drawbacks and can lead to adverse outcomes, the field is advancing rapidly. The advent of generative AI marks a significant leap in our ability to infuse intelligence into various facets of the world.

This continuous advancement, coupled with the development of diverse applications, positions AI as a critical contributor to longer, healthier, and more fulfilling lives globally. As we forge ahead, improving AI technology and expanding its use cases, the concerns that alarm us today will likely diminish, much like the fears associated with electricity did. Ng's perspective offers a hopeful outlook on the future of AI, underscoring its potential to bring about transformative changes akin to those brought by electricity.

As we finish reading this book, consider some essential questions about artificial intelligence. We wonder if AI will ever become conscious and if achieving Artificial General Intelligence (AGI) will happen soon. Only time will answer these questions, opening up endless possibilities for the unwritten future.

Furthermore, we cannot overstate the impact of Generative AI on productivity. It harbors the potential to contribute trillions of dollars to the global economy, marking a significant milestone in the evolution of our economic structures. This transformative power of AI is not just a speculative idea; it is a burgeoning reality, reshaping industries and redefining productivity parameters.

In this context, it is imperative to acknowledge that indifference to this seismic shift may have profound implications. If you remain unresponsive to the advancements in AI, there lies a tangible risk of being overshadowed by those who embrace and understand these technologies. The future will likely favor those alert to the winds of change, adapting and evolving with the tide of AI innovation.

The concluding thought, therefore, is one of caution and optimism. It is a call to action for proactive engagement with AI. By understanding and leveraging the potential of AI, we can not only safeguard our professional relevance but also contribute to and benefit from the vast economic and societal enhancements it promises. The winners in this era of rapid technological change will be those who choose not to remain indifferent but actively engage with and adapt to the evolving landscape of artificial intelligence.

In conclusion, we should adopt a proactive and optimistic stance rather than succumbing to fear or indifference toward artificial intelligence. AI, like electricity in its early days, promises transformative change in various aspects of our lives. As we witness the continuous advancements in AI, it becomes evident that the initial concerns and challenges can be addressed and mitigated. By actively engaging with AI, understanding its capabilities, and adapting to its evolving landscape, we position ourselves to thrive and contribute to the significant societal and economic improvements it offers. The future belongs to those who embrace AI's opportunities and participate in shaping the promising path ahead.

Yesterday is history,
Tomorrow is a mystery,
Today is a gift, that's why it's called the present.

Alice Morse Earle
American historian and writer

SUGGESTED READINGS: Articles published by the authors

- [ ] Neural Networks And Multivariate Statistical Methods In Traffic Accident Modeling (2010) - Erzincan University Journal of Science and Technology - Dr. F.Hattatoglu

- [ ] Different Methods For The Modelling Of Traffic Accidents Prediction Of Erzincan Province (2011) - Erzincan University Journal of Science and Technology - Dr. F.Hattatoglu

- [ ] The Effects of Artificial Intelligence and Robotic Systems on Librarianship (2018) – Türk Kütüphaneciliği - M.Yildiz

- [ ] Claude 2.1 Achieves Remarkable Honesty: Hallucination Rates Reduced by 2x! (2023) - Medium - M.Yildiz

- [ ] Algorithm of Thoughts (AoT) and the Development of Artificial Intelligence's Reasoning Ability (2023) - Medium - Dr. F.Hattatoglu

- [ ] Prompt Engineering Formulas For ChatGPT and Other Language Models (2023) - Medium - Dr. F.Hattatoglu

- [ ] Unlocking Generative AI: Impressions from Andrew Ng's 'Generative AI for Everyone' Course by DeepLearning.AI (2023) - Medium - M.Yildiz

- [ ] What's Behind ChatGPT! (2023)- Medium - M.Yildiz

- ☐ ETL Process on Data Science (2023) - Medium - Dr. F.Hattatoglu

- ☐ Bringing it to life: Deployment with Streamlit (2023) - Medium - Dr. F.Hattatoglu

- ☐ The complexity of the human brain and its relationship with artificial intelligence: ANN, RNN, LSTM and GRU (2023) - Medium - M.Yildiz

- ☐ Artificial Intelligence Touch to Google Sheets: Integration of GPT (2023) - Medium - M.Yildiz

- ☐ A Top 5 Soft Skill: Analytical Thinking and Mind Mapping as its Application Method (2023) - Medium - Dr. F.Hattatoglu

REFERENCES

Abraham, A. (2005). Artificial neural networks. Handbook of measuring system design.

Agathokleous, E., Saitanis, C. J., Fang, C., & Yu, Z. (2023). Use of ChatGPT: What does it mean for biology and environmental science?. Science of The Total Environment, 888, 164154.

Ausat, A. M. A., Massang, B., Efendi, M., Nofirman, N., & Riady, Y. (2023). Can chat GPT replace the role of the teacher in the classroom: A fundamental analysis. Journal on Education, 5(4), 16100-16106.

Bahdanau, D., Cho, K., & Bengio, Y. (2014). Neural machine translation by jointly learning to align and translate. arXiv preprint arXiv:1409.0473.

Baidoo-Anu, D., & Ansah, L. O. (2023). Education in the era of generative artificial intelligence (AI): Understanding the potential benefits of ChatGPT in promoting teaching and learning. Journal of AI, 7(1), 52-62.

Banerjee, D., Singh, P., Avadhanam, A., & Srivastava, S. (2023). Benchmarking LLM powered Chatbots: Methods and Metrics. arXiv preprint arXiv:2308.04624.

Barto, A. G. (1997). Reinforcement learning. In Neural systems for control (pp. 7-30). Academic Press.

Basheer, I. A., & Hajmeer, M. (2000). Artificial neural networks: fundamentals, computing, design, and application. Journal of microbiological methods, 43(1), 3-31.

Belgati, B. (2023). WTH is Prompt Engineering?
https://dev.to/pavanbelagatti/wth-is-prompt-engineering-h03

Bengio, Y., Simard, P., & Frasconi, P. (1994). Learning long-term dependencies with gradient descent is difficult. IEEE transactions on neural networks, 5(2), 157-166.

Biswas, S. (2023a). Role of Chat GPT in Education. Available at SSRN 4369981.

Biswas, S. (2023b). Role of chat gpt in public health. Annals of biomedical engineering, 51(5), 868-869.

Bommasani, R., Hudson, D. A., Adeli, E., Altman, R., Arora, S., von Arx, S., ... & Liang, P. (2021). On the opportunities and risks of foundation models. arXiv preprint arXiv:2108.07258.

Borgeaud, S., Mensch, A., Hoffmann, J., Cai, T., Rutherford, E., Millican, K., ... & Sifre, L. (2022, June). Improving language models by retrieving from trillions of tokens. In International conference on machine learning (pp. 2206-2240). PMLR.

Brown, T., Mann, B., Ryder, N., Subbiah, M., Kaplan, J. D., Dhariwal, P., ... & Amodei, D. (2020). Language models are few-shot learners. Advances in neural information processing systems, 33, 1877-1901.

Cai, X. (2021). The Evolution of the Convolutional Neural Networks Architecture. https://www.lablab.top/post/the-evolution-of-the-convolutional-neural-networks-architecture/

Cao, Y., Li, S., Liu, Y., Yan, Z., Dai, Y., Yu, P. S., & Sun, L. (2023). A comprehensive survey of ai-generated content (aigc): A history of generative ai from gan to chatgpt. arXiv preprint arXiv:2303.04226.

Casper, S., Davies, X., Shi, C., Gilbert, T. K., Scheurer, J., Rando, J., ... & Hadfield-Menell, D. (2023). Open problems and fundamental limitations of reinforcement learning from human feedback. arXiv preprint arXiv:2307.15217.

Cho, K., Van Merriënboer, B., Bahdanau, D., & Bengio, Y. (2014). On the properties of neural machine translation: Encoder-decoder approaches. arXiv preprint arXiv:1409.1259.

Chui, M., Hazan, E., Roberts, R., Singla, A., & Smaje, K. (2023). The economic potential of generative AI.The next productivity frontier.

Chung, J., Gulcehre, C., Cho, K., & Bengio, Y. (2014). Empirical evaluation of gated recurrent neural networks on sequence modeling. arXiv preprint arXiv:1412.3555.

Conwell, C., & Ullman, T. (2022). Testing relational understanding in text-guided image generation. arXiv preprint arXiv:2208.00005.

Dai, W., Liu, Z., Ji, Z., Su, D., & Fung, P. (2022). Plausible may not be faithful: Probing object hallucination in vision-language pre-training. arXiv preprint arXiv:2210.07688.

Databricks. (2023). Large Language Models. https://www.databricks.com/product/machine-learning/large-language-models

Deep Learning.AI. (2023). Generative AI for Everyone. https://www.deeplearning.ai/courses/generative-ai-for-everyone/

Devlin, J., Chang, M. W., Lee, K., & Toutanova, K. (2018). Bert: Pre-training of deep bidirectional transformers for language understanding. arXiv preprint arXiv:1810.04805.

Eddy, S. R. (2004). What is a hidden Markov model?. Nature biotechnology, 22(10), 1315-1316.

Ewald, J. (2023). Introduction to Large Language Models. Google Cloud Tech. https://www.youtube.com/watch?v=zizonToFXDs&t=41s.

Foster, D. (2019). Generative Deep Learning. Teaching Machines to Paint, Write, Compose and Play (2019). Beijing-Boston-Farnham-Sebastopol-Tokyo, OREILLY, 330.

François-Lavet, V., Henderson, P., Islam, R., Bellemare, M. G., & Pineau, J. (2018). An introduction to deep reinforcement learning. Foundations and Trends® in Machine Learning, 11(3-4), 219-354.

Fui-Hoon Nah, F., Zheng, R., Cai, J., Siau, K., & Chen, L. (2023). Generative AI and ChatGPT: Applications, challenges, and AI-human collaboration. Journal of Information Technology Case and Application Research, 25(3), 277-304.

Gartner (2023). What is Generative AI? the Future of GenAI. https://www.gartner.com/en/insights/generative-ai-for-business

Gers, F. A., Schmidhuber, J., & Cummins, F. (2000). Learning to forget: Continual prediction with LSTM. Neural computation, 12(10), 2451-2471.

Giray, L. (2023). Prompt Engineering with ChatGPT: A Guide for Academic Writers. Annals of Biomedical Engineering, 1-5.

Goodfellow, I. J. (2014). On distinguishability criteria for estimating generative models. arXiv preprint arXiv:1412.6515.

Grossberg, S. (2013). Recurrent neural networks. Scholarpedia, 8(2), 1888.

Guerreiro, N. M., Alves, D., Waldendorf, J., Haddow, B., Birch, A., Colombo, P., & Martins, A. F. (2023). Hallucinations in large multilingual translation models. arXiv preprint arXiv:2303.16104.

Guu, K., Lee, K., Tung, Z., Pasupat, P., & Chang, M. (2020, November). Retrieval augmented language model pre-training. In International conference on machine learning (pp. 3929-3938). PMLR.

Hatzius, J. (2023). The Potentially Large Effects of Artificial Intelligence on Economic Growth (Briggs/Kodnani). Goldman Sachs.

Henrickson, L., & Meroño-Peñuela, A. (2023). Prompting meaning: a hermeneutic approach to optimizing prompt engineering with ChatGPT. AI & SOCIETY, 1-16.

Hochreiter, S. (1991). Untersuchungen zu dynamischen neuronalen Netzen. Diploma, Technische Universität München, 91(1), 31.

Hochreiter, S., & Schmidhuber, J. (1997). LSTM can solve hard long time lag problems. Advances in neural information processing systems, 9.

Hopfield, J. J. (1988). Artificial neural networks. IEEE Circuits and Devices Magazine, 4(5), 3-10.

Hu, K. (2023). ChatGPT sets record for fastest-growing user base-analyst note. Reuters, 12, 2023.

Huang, L., Yu, W., Ma, W., Zhong, W., Feng, Z., Wang, H., ... & Liu, T. (2023). A survey on hallucination in large language models: Principles, taxonomy, challenges, and open questions. arXiv preprint arXiv:2311.05232.

Huang, Z., Yang, F., Xu, F., Song, X., & Tsui, K. L. (2019). Convolutional gated recurrent unit–recurrent neural network for state-of-charge estimation of lithium-ion batteries. Ieee Access, 7, 93139-93149.

Izacard, G., Lewis, P., Lomeli, M., Hosseini, L., Petroni, F., Schick, T., ... & Grave, E. (2022). Few-shot learning with retrieval augmented language models. arXiv preprint arXiv:2208.03299.

Jenkins, I. R., Gee, L. O., Knauss, A., Yin, H., & Schroeder, J. (2018, November). Accident scenario generation with recurrent neural networks. In 2018 21st International Conference on Intelligent Transportation Systems (ITSC) (pp. 3340-3345). IEEE.

Ji, Z., Lee, N., Frieske, R., Yu, T., Su, D., Xu, Y., ... & Fung, P. (2023). Survey of hallucination in natural language generation. ACM Computing Surveys, 55(12), 1-38.

Jiang, Z., Xu, F. F., Gao, L., Sun, Z., Liu, Q., Dwivedi-Yu, J., ... & Neubig, G. (2023). Active retrieval augmented generation. arXiv preprint arXiv:2305.06983.

Kapelyukh, I., Vosylius, V., & Johns, E. (2023). Dall-e-bot: Introducing web-scale diffusion models to robotics. IEEE Robotics and Automation Letters.

Karpathy, A. (2023). Intro to Large Language Models. Youtube video. https://www.youtube.com/watch?v=zjkBMFhNj_g

Kasneci, E., Seßler, K., Küchemann, S., Bannert, M., Dementieva, D., Fischer, F., ... & Kasneci, G. (2023). ChatGPT for good? On opportunities and challenges of large language models for education. Learning and individual differences, 103, 102274.

Khattab et al. (2021). Building Scalable, Explainable, and Adaptive NLP Models with Retrieval.https://ai.stanford.edu/blog/retrieval-based-NLP/

Kojima, T., Gu, S. S., Reid, M., Matsuo, Y., & Iwasawa, Y. (2022). Large language models are zero-shot reasoners. Advances in neural information processing systems, 35, 22199-22213.

Krenker, A., Bešter, J., & Kos, A. (2011). Introduction to the artificial neural networks. Artificial Neural Networks: Methodological Advances and Biomedical Applications. InTech, 1-18.

Lapata, M. (2023). What is generative AI and how does it work? https://www.youtube.com/watch?v=_6R7Ym6Vy_I

Lee, H., Phatale, S., Mansoor, H., Lu, K., Mesnard, T., Bishop, C., ... & Rastogi, A. (2023). Rlaif: Scaling reinforcement learning from human feedback with ai feedback. arXiv preprint arXiv:2309.00267.

LeCun, Y. (1998). The MNIST database of handwritten digits. http://yann. lecun. com/exdb/mnist/.

Leivada, E., Murphy, E., & Marcus, G. (2023). DALL· E 2 fails to reliably capture common syntactic processes. Social Sciences & Humanities Open, 8(1), 100648.

Levy, D., & Rector-Brooks, J. (2023, May). Molecular Fragment-based Diffusion Model for Drug Discovery. In ICLR 2023-Machine Learning for Drug Discovery workshop.

Lewis, P., Perez, E., Piktus, A., Petroni, F., Karpukhin, V., Goyal, N., ... & Kiela, D. (2020). Retrieval-augmented generation for knowledge-intensive nlp tasks. Advances in Neural Information Processing Systems, 33, 9459-9474.

Li, Y. (2017). Deep reinforcement learning: An overview. arXiv preprint arXiv:1701.07274.

LifeArchitect (2023). 2023-2024 Optimal Language Models. https://lifearchitect.ai/models/

Lim, W. M., Gunasekara, A., Pallant, J. L., Pallant, J. I., & Pechenkina, E. (2023). Generative AI and the future of education: Ragnarök or reformation? A paradoxical perspective from management educators. The International Journal of Management Education, 21(2), 100790.

Lin, T., Wang, Y., Liu, X., & Qiu, X. (2022). A survey of transformers. AI Open.

Lin, X. V., Chen, X., Chen, M., Shi, W., Lomeli, M., James, R., ... & Yih, S. (2023). RA-DIT: Retrieval-Augmented Dual Instruction Tuning. arXiv preprint arXiv:2310.01352.

Liu, P., Yuan, W., Fu, J., Jiang, Z., Hayashi, H., & Neubig, G. (2023a). Pre-train, prompt, and predict: A systematic survey of prompting methods in natural language processing. ACM Computing Surveys, 55(9), 1-35.

Liu, Y., Han, T., Ma, S., Zhang, J., Yang, Y., Tian, J., ... & Ge, B. (2023b). Summary of chatgpt-related research and perspective towards the future of large language models. Meta-Radiology, 100017.

Liu, G. K. M. (2023). Perspectives on the Social Impacts of Reinforcement Learning with Human Feedback. arXiv preprint arXiv:2303.02891.

Lund, B., & Agbaji, D. (2023). Information literacy, data literacy, privacy literacy, and chatgpt: Technology literacies align with perspectives on emerging technology adoption within communities. Data Literacy, Privacy Literacy, and ChatGPT: Technology Literacies Align with Perspectives on Emerging Technology Adoption within Communities (January 14, 2023).

Mannuru, N. R., Shahriar, S., Teel, Z. A., Wang, T., Lund, B. D., Tijani, S., ... & Vaidya, P. (2023). Artificial intelligence in developing countries: The impact of generative artificial intelligence (AI) technologies for development. Information Development, 02666669231200628.

Marcus, G., Davis, E., & Aaronson, S. (2022). A very preliminary analysis of DALL-E 2. arXiv preprint arXiv:2204.13807.

Maynez, J., Narayan, S., Bohnet, B., & McDonald, R. (2020). On faithfulness and factuality in abstractive summarization. arXiv preprint arXiv:2005.00661.

McKinsey (2023). The economic potential of generative AI: The next productivity frontier. https://www.mckinsey.com/capabilities/mckinsey-digital/our-insights/the-economic-potential-of-generative-ai-the-next-productivity-frontier#key-insights

Medsker, L. R., & Jain, L. C. (2001). Recurrent neural networks. Design and Applications, 5(64-67), 2.

Meskó, B., & Topol, E. J. (2023). The imperative for regulatory oversight of large language models (or generative AI) in healthcare. npj Digital Medicine, 6(1), 120.

Mirchandani, S., Xia, F., Florence, P., Ichter, B., Driess, D., Arenas, M. G., ... & Zeng, A. (2023). Large language models as general pattern machines. arXiv preprint arXiv:2307.04721.

MIT Technology Review Insights (2023). Finding value in generative AI for financial services. 26 November 2023.

Moor, M., Banerjee, O., Abad, Z. S. H., Krumholz, H. M., Leskovec, J., Topol, E. J., & Rajpurkar, P. (2023). Foundation models for generalist medical artificial intelligence. Nature, 616(7956), 259-265.

O'Connor (2022). Introduction to Diffusion Models for Machine Learning. https://www.assemblyai.com/blog/diffusion-models-for-machine-learning-introduction/

Olah, C. (2015). Understanding LSTM Networks. http://colah.github.io/posts/2015-08-Understanding-LSTMs/

Orchard, T., & Tasiemski, L. (2023). The rise of Generative AI and possible effects on the economy. Economics and Business Review, 9(2), 9-26.

Ouyang, L., Wu, J., Jiang, X., Almeida, D., Wainwright, C., Mishkin, P., ... & Lowe, R. (2022). Training language models to follow instructions with human feedback. Advances in Neural Information Processing Systems, 35, 27730-27744.

Priddy, K. L., & Keller, P. E. (2005). Artificial neural networks: an introduction (Vol. 68). SPIE press.

Rabiner, L., & Juang, B. (1986). An introduction to hidden Markov models. ieee assp magazine, 3(1), 4-16.

Radhakrishnan, A., Nguyen, K., Chen, A., Chen, C., Denison, C., Hernandez, D., ... & Perez, E. (2023). Question decomposition improves the faithfulness of model-generated reasoning. arXiv preprint arXiv:2307.11768.

Ram, O., Levine, Y., Dalmedigos, I., Muhlgay, D., Shashua, A., Leyton-Brown, K., & Shoham, Y. (2023). In-context retrieval-augmented language models. arXiv preprint arXiv:2302.00083.

Ramesh, A., Dhariwal, P., Nichol, A., Chu, C., & Chen, M. (2022). Hierarchical text-conditional image generation with clip latents. arXiv preprint arXiv:2204.06125, 1(2), 3.

Ramlochan, S. (2023). What is Prompt Engineering? https://promptengineering.org/what-is-prompt-engineering/

Rashkin, H., Reitter, D., Tomar, G. S., & Das, D. (2021). Increasing faithfulness in knowledge-grounded dialogue with controllable features. arXiv preprint arXiv:2107.06963.

Rawte, V., Priya, P., Tonmoy, S. M., Zaman, S. M., Sheth, A., & Das, A. (2023a). Exploring the relationship between LLM hallucinations and prompt linguistic nuances: Readability, formality, and concreteness. arXiv preprint arXiv:2309.11064.

Rawte, V., Sheth, A., & Das, A. (2023b). A survey of hallucination in large foundation models. arXiv preprint arXiv:2309.05922.

Ren, R., Wang, Y., Qu, Y., Zhao, W. X., Liu, J., Tian, H., ... & Wang, H. (2023). Investigating the factual knowledge boundary of large language models with retrieval augmentation. arXiv preprint arXiv:2307.11019.

Rombach, R., Blattmann, A., Lorenz, D., Esser, P., & Ommer, B. (2022). High-resolution image synthesis with latent diffusion models. In Proceedings of the IEEE/CVF conference on computer vision and pattern recognition (pp. 10684-10695).

Qader, W. A., Ameen, M. M., & Ahmed, B. I. (2019, June). An overview of the bag of words; importance, implementation, applications, and challenges. In 2019 international engineering conference (IEC) (pp. 200-204). IEEE.

Qin, Y., Hu, S., Lin, Y., Chen, W., Ding, N., Cui, G., ... & Sun, M. (2023). Tool learning with foundation models. arXiv preprint arXiv:2304.08354.

Salehinejad, H., Sankar, S., Barfett, J., Colak, E., & Valaee, S. (2017). Recent advances in recurrent neural networks. arXiv preprint arXiv:1801.01078.

Sebastian, G. (2023). Do ChatGPT and other AI chatbots pose a cybersecurity risk?: An exploratory study. International Journal of Security and Privacy in Pervasive Computing (IJSPPC), 15(1), 1-11.

Sharma, R. (2023). How to Connect LLM to External Sources Using RAG?. https://markovate.com/blog/connect-llm-using-rag/

Sherstinsky, A. (2020). Fundamentals of recurrent neural network (RNN) and long short-term memory (LSTM) network. Physica D: Nonlinear Phenomena, 404, 132306.

Shewalkar, A., Nyavanandi, D., & Ludwig, S. A. (2019). Performance evaluation of deep neural networks applied to speech recognition: RNN, LSTM and GRU. Journal of Artificial Intelligence and Soft Computing Research, 9(4), 235-245.

Shi, W., Min, S., Yasunaga, M., Seo, M., James, R., Lewis, M., ... & Yih, W. T. (2023). Replug: Retrieval-augmented black-box language models. arXiv preprint arXiv:2301.12652.

Short, C. E., & Short, J. C. (2023). The artificially intelligent entrepreneur: ChatGPT, prompt engineering, and entrepreneurial rhetoric creation. Journal of Business Venturing Insights, 19, e00388.

Silverstein, S. (1981). A Light in the Attic. Harper & Row.

Stripling, G. (2023). Introduction to Generative AI. Google Cloud Tech, https://www.youtube.com/watch?v=G2fqAlgmoPo.

Sutton, R. S., & Barto, A. G. (1999). Reinforcement learning. Journal of Cognitive Neuroscience, 11(1), 126-134.

Sutton, R. S., & Barto, A. G. (2018). Reinforcement learning: An introduction. MIT press.

Thirunavukarasu, A. J., Ting, D. S. J., Elangovan, K., Gutierrez, L., Tan, T. F., & Ting, D. S. W. (2023). Large language models in medicine. Nature medicine, 29(8), 1930-1940.

Turing, A. M. (1950). Mind. Mind, 59(236), 433-460.

Xu, Y., Kong, D., Xu, D., Ji, Z., Pang, B., Fung, P., & Wu, Y. N. (2023). Diverse and Faithful Knowledge-Grounded Dialogue Generation via Sequential Posterior Inference. arXiv preprint arXiv:2306.01153.

Vaswani, A., Shazeer, N., Parmar, N., Uszkoreit, J., Jones, L., Gomez, A. N., ... & Polosukhin, I. (2017). Attention is all you need. Advances in neural information processing systems, 30.

Welsh, M.(2023). Large Language Models and The End of Programming - CS50 Tech Talk with Dr. Matt Welsh.
Youtube: https://www.youtube.com/watch?v=JhCl-GeT4jw&t=1255s

White, J., Fu, Q., Hays, S., Sandborn, M., Olea, C., Gilbert, H., ... & Schmidt, D. C. (2023). A prompt pattern catalog to enhance prompt engineering with chatgpt. arXiv preprint arXiv:2302.11382.

Wiering, M. A., & Van Otterlo, M. (2012). Reinforcement learning. Adaptation, learning, and optimization, 12(3), 729.

Wolf, T., Debut, L., Sanh, V., Chaumond, J., Delangue, C., Moi, A., ... & Rush, A. M. (2020, October). Transformers: State-of-the-art natural language processing. In Proceedings of the 2020 conference on empirical methods in natural language processing: system demonstrations (pp. 38-45).

Wolfram, S. (2023). What is ChatGPT Doing...and Why Does It Work? https://writings.stephenwolfram.com/2023/02/what-is-chatgpt-doing-and-why-does-it-work/

Wu, Y., Rabe, M. N., Hutchins, D., & Szegedy, C. (2022). Memorizing transformers. arXiv preprint arXiv:2203.08913.

Yang, S., Nachum, O., Du, Y., Wei, J., Abbeel, P., & Schuurmans, D. (2023). Foundation models for decision making: Problems, methods, and opportunities. arXiv preprint arXiv:2303.04129.

Yao, J. Y., Ning, K. P., Liu, Z. H., Ning, M. N., & Yuan, L. (2023). Llm lies: Hallucinations are not bugs, but features as adversarial examples. arXiv preprint arXiv:2310.01469.

Yasungaga, M. (2023). RA-CM3: Retrieval-Augmented Multimodel Modeling. https://cs.stanford.edu/~myasu/blog/racm3/#background-retrieval-augmentation

Yegnanarayana, B. (2009). Artificial neural networks. PHI Learning Pvt. Ltd.

Yin, Z., Sun, Q., Guo, Q., Wu, J., Qiu, X., & Huang, X. (2023). Do Large Language Models Know What They Don't Know?. arXiv preprint arXiv:2305.18153.

Zhang, Y., Jin, R., & Zhou, Z. H. (2010). Understanding bag-of-words model: a statistical framework. International journal of machine learning and cybernetics, 1, 43-52.

Zhang, Z., Jia, M., Yao, B., Das, S., Lerner, A., Wang, D., & Li, T. (2023a). " It's a Fair Game", or Is It? Examining How Users Navigate Disclosure Risks and Benefits When Using LLM-Based Conversational Agents. arXiv preprint arXiv:2309.11653.

Zhang, Y., Li, Y., Cui, L., Cai, D., Liu, L., Fu, T., ... & Shi, S. (2023b). Siren's Song in the AI Ocean: A Survey on Hallucination in Large Language Models. arXiv preprint arXiv:2309.01219.

Zhao, W. X., Zhou, K., Li, J., Tang, T., Wang, X., Hou, Y., ... & Wen, J. R. (2023a). A survey of large language models. arXiv preprint arXiv:2303.18223.

Zhao, R., Chen, H., Wang, W., Jiao, F., Do, X. L., Qin, C., ... & Joty, S. (2023b). Retrieving multimodal information for augmented generation: A survey. arXiv preprint arXiv:2303.10868.

Zhou, C., Li, Q., Li, C., Yu, J., Liu, Y., Wang, G., ... & Sun, L. (2023). A comprehensive survey on pretrained foundation models: A history from bert to chatgpt. arXiv preprint arXiv:2302.09419.

Zhu, B., Jiao, J., & Jordan, M. I. (2023). Principled Reinforcement Learning with Human Feedback from Pairwise or K-wise Comparisons. arXiv preprint arXiv:2301.11270.

Zou, J., Han, Y., & So, S. S. (2009). Overview of artificial neural networks. Artificial neural networks: methods and applications, 14-22.

Printed in Great Britain
by Amazon